Tastefully Twisted Publications

In Cooperation with

Tastefully Twisted Politics

Proudly Presents

The Top Ten American Political Myths

So…What exactly is a "Political Myth" you ask? I'm glad you brought this up. Let's spend some time together and discuss it, shall we?

A "Political Myth" is just all other forms of mythology; stories that while having maybe been at one time based in fact, have been so distorted by its continually growing distance from its original factual source material, it bears little resemblance at all to any factual nature the concept upon which the myth is based is completely gone. To simply state the point in something other than a "Run-On Sentence," it's something that may have started out with a hint of truth to it; but has completely devolved into bullshit.

To say that this can be frustrating is…well…frustratingly inaccurate. I've been politically active; or at least interested for a pretty good while now. And where I still believe being "Involved" is an overall noble pursuit, there have been more than a few times that I've become so frustrated by examples of pure ignorance in political debate, I've wanted to never discuss American politics again. Indeed there have been times when I actually have sworn off political debate; but have changed my mind because I felt that the information I either already possessed or knew where to find was important enough to "Put out there." Similarly, I've felt that positions that I either have or strongly support are important enough to argue to the best of my ability.

Without any doubt, the biggest source of frustration is the often ridiculous information that many Conservatives actually believe and the political and social positions those same Conservatives believe that Progressives support.

Much of the information of which I speak are not much more than misconceptions that are easily dispelled. Examples of these include, "Liberals want to significantly raise taxes (Upwards of 40 to 50%)," or "All Liberals are Atheists."

Under President Obama's administration, there have been across the board tax cuts that, although not appearing significant, have prevented inflation from causing the actual dollar amounts to rise noticeably.

In addition, just like Republicans, most Democrats claim to be Evangelical Christians; at least in being aligned with the general principles of Evangelical Christianity.

What causes me the most frustration though, are the utterly ridiculous things that too many Conservatives honestly believe American Progressives either believe in or are making a concerted effort to make happen. These range between being indicative of severe mental illness, to "Where in the hell did you pull that crap out of??"

Some of the ludicrous things Conservatives believe about Progressives defy logic and rationality so much that one can't help but think that they're jokes. "Pulling the plug on Gramma," "Seizing the assets of the rich, selling them and then giving the cash to America's poor" sound really funny at first.

But just like the lecture of a University Professor beginning with, "The first thing you have to understand about Religious History is that the Earth is only six thousand years old;" at some point one comes to the horrible realization, "My God…he's serious!"

Even more frustrating, even to the point of being painfully disheartening is the all-too frequent reality that, even after being informed as to the factual nature of Progressive political ideology and/or actual Progressive political and social policy, seemingly intelligent people will make the conscious decision to believe in even the most insane misleading information. In my own lifetime, I've seen some otherwise bright people choose to believe utter nonsense, knowing full well that the information they're choosing to believe is inaccurate.

The worst examples are, of course those times when one or more people that some Conservatives are allowing to spoon feed them are caught in bold-faced lies and still believe the falsehoods they've been fed; justifying their choices by disconnecting from facts through adopting beliefs based on the "True Nature" of Progressive ideology.

The classic example of this is, of course answering the factual nature of President Obama not once even hinting at wanting to overturn the Second Amendment with, "It's still what he wants to do."

Over the course of the last year, I've made an effort to stem the tide of this voluntary ignorance by exposing political "BS" wherever I find it; even exposing Progressive "BS" when I've found it.

In addition, I've commented on inaccurate political posts made by friends and acquaintances with the facts about the "BS" they believe and in many of these attempts, I've received very strong reactions from those who want the inaccuracies being shoved down their throats to be true so badly, they've seen my commentary as a personal insult.

My main purpose for putting out the information I've shared has been not so much to change people's minds; but more for the purpose of achieving the goal of real dialogue in important political matters. I strongly believe that the greatest obstacle to any kind of political progress is those representing political positions not talking to each other on equal terms.

This factor of American politics is a direct result of inaccurate information being chosen over facts. This is extremely frustrating as this, not only makes intelligent discussion difficult at best, it really makes those choosing the inaccuracies (And I feel I have to be painfully honest here) look kinda stupid.

How can one side talk with another side if that other side is in essence isn't even discussing the same topic? This is what the gun debate has devolved into as Progressives trying to argue the merits of a measure such as "Denying the sale of firearms to people on terrorist watch lists" inevitably and without fail being confronted with the familiar arguments against "Banning guns in America."

At times, it's been like trying to have a conversation with a tape recorder that someone just dropped off and pressed "Play." It only gets worse when the discussion inevitably degrades to the point of popular catch phrases being tossed into the discussion; such as the tried and true "Guns Don't Kill People, People Kill People;" which I personally feel is a metaphorical spit in the face.

The message put across with this argument strategy is, "I am NOT going to try and discuss this matter with you on an equal basis." It also delivers the message, "This is pretty much all I got;" once more making one look like a moron.

At this point, I think I should at least mention that I am well aware that there are imbeciles on my side as well. Similarly, there are people out there that are so unbelievably far to the "Left" they make me look tame by comparison.

But unlike the relationships between Conservative ideology and people like Ted Nugent and Sarah Palin, we tend to not take them as seriously. Today, there are a lot more people asking Michael Moore, "Can you please just go away?" than taking anything he says or writes seriously (He REALLY cheesed us off with the whole, "Don't send aid to Michigan" crap.).

So no...we do not want to take away your freedom of speech with "Political Correctness." We don't want to evict a wealthy family from their Beverly Hills mansion and replace them with a family that "Decorates" their lawns with twenty year old Buicks that they're "Gonna fix someday." We're not giving a thousand dollars cash to every "Illegal Immigrant" who crosses the border. We're not persecuting Christians. We don't want to establish a government agency that decides which Americans will be gay or straight whether they like it or not (I'm not kidding. I've actually heard this). And for the love of Pete Sampras, we are NOT coming for your guns.

Have any further questions about Progressive sociopolitical ideology, ask a liberal. We'll be glad to answer any of your questions and we'll try not to laugh at some of the more bizarre things you've been led to believe.

If you're not willing to understand what we really believe and/or want to accomplish, then please don't engage us in a conversation that will only result in the loss of a period of time that we can't have back.

Top 10 American Political Myths #10

All Criticism and Opposition to the Policies of President Barack Obama is Based on Racism Specifically Focused on the President himself.

President Obama is not the first American President to face opposition or criticism as a result of racist or discriminatory ideology. Extremists in both the Republican and Democratic Party urged people to vote against eventual President John F. Kennedy and Senator Robert Kennedy's campaigns based only on the fact that both were Irish and Catholic.

President Lyndon Johnson faced opposition from the Southern office holders and candidates in his own party and from Republicans who were committed to Barry Goldwater's open opposition to Johnson's Civil Rights agenda.

Ironically, candidate and eventual President Richard M. Nixon was opposed by intellectual elitists who looked down on him for his, mostly public education.

But all of this would pale in comparison to the fierce opposition President Obama has faced in his tenure behind the desk in the Oval Office. Virtually every piece of legislation he has supported has been blocked by a Republican Party that, very quickly developed the reputation as "The Party of No."

The general obstructionist policy of the Republican Party didn't start in 2011 when the GOP took back control of the House of Representatives (Can we please stop referring to "The House" as Congress? The term "Congress" is supposed to represent both "The House" AND the Senate). It was merely exacerbated by the fact that those same Republicans were, since the ones who in control. With Democrats retaining a small majority in the Senate, this would lead to an unprecedented era of stagnation in U.S. Government; punctuated by government shutdowns, financial crises and the credit rating of the U.S. being damaged in a way that probably won't change...for a while.

I believe that it should be pointed out that both of President Obama's terms have been characterized by racial tensions not seen since the 1960s. However, while many of the President's critics have pointed to him being the originator of these tensions by "Playing the Race Card;" there is considerable evidence that points to the source of the tension being racially-related issues unresolved since the 1960s.

These unresolved issues boiled over after the public scrutiny of African-Americans killed by "White" police officers in various ways. This irritated the unhealed wounds that had quietly been festering involving African-American communities generally distrustful of police and law enforcement assigned to patrol mostly African-American neighborhoods.

It has been typical of American history that more "White" people join Police Departments than any other demographic. And while most crime in America occurs in impoverished neighborhoods; there are a disproportionate number of poor African-American neighborhoods than "White" due to Civil Rights legislation passed in the 1960s being slow to result in economic advancement of African-American communities.

And while President Obama may not be the factual cause of racial tensions in America; every President has and likely always will be looked upon as being; not only responsible for the good and bad of what is happening during their era; but in history as well.

President Obama may have nothing to do with the actual socially historical moments of his Presidency; but the perception that he is responsible and history remembering him for them comes with the job.

On a personal note; I don't believe that President Obama could have been naive to the point of not knowing this before handing out his first "Hope" campaign buttons in 2008; and certainly not in his second campaign.

So racial tensions did start to boil over during the current administration's era. Does this mean that open racism is behind any and all opposition and/or criticism of it? In a word: No…at least not in the way people easily identify.

Some of the ludicrous double standards applied to his Presidency do feature a hint of the scent of prejudice; but these are more likely to be based on old political grudges seeping into American politics. Evidence of this can be seen in, at least one of the double standards being applied to Former Secretary of State Hillary Clinton's campaign by a rival Democratic challenger.

Senator Bernie Sanders didn't seem to mind "Special Interests" and "Wall Street" money being essential to the campaigns of President Bill Clinton or President Obama. However, accusations of "Selling Out to Special Interests" dominated his campaign against Former Secretary Clinton's.

In addition, here in Texas accusations of "Corruption" and "Abuse of Power" haven't hurt Former Governor Rick Perry very much. Fortunately, it appears that; so far at least, Donald Trump has been smart enough to not play that card; though he hasn't made any effort to stop any of his supporters from "Going There."

It is also fortunate that the looming threat of future attacks against her own integrity have effectively prevented Former Secretary Clinton from pulling that out of her political portfolio. (And yes! This progressive voter thinks this is a good thing.)

So...partisan political grudges being more the culprit of ludicrous double standards is far more likely to be a factor than open racism? I believe that to be much more reasonable. And political stupidity is not always racist in nature. More often, it's just plain stupidity.

A politician taking the Bible out of context or a minister giving the strong impression of praying for the death of the U.S. President is more likely just a severely inappropriate joke than open racism. In addition, virtually every example of political stupidity I could list has arguably hurt the Republican cause than helped it. Perceiving a political candidate as racist has historically not been more damaging than the perception that the same candidate being a moron.

And, of course there is the arguably much more legitimate factor of the President's political agenda being contrary to the nature of Conservative political ideology. Major changes in programs like Social Security, Medicare and food programs stem from differences in political thought. The NRA's campaigns against the President are based more on the myth that the President intends to overturn the Second Amendment have virtually nothing to do with the color of the current President's skin; but rather on the fear generated by a populace that elected him. After all, if traditional "White" values have been rejected in the image of a White President; what else is the "New Order" willing to reject?

There are, of course millions of people who believe that the President is unqualified solely based on his race; but these idiots are (Thankfully) more on the fringes of the political arena; much more the proverbial "Exception than the Rule."

Yes, racial tensions have come to a head during the President's terms; and justly or not, his Presidency will be forever marked for them. Again...this comes with the paycheck. Even if President Obama were to come down to my house, sit in the office chair (The recliner's MINE!) and lament to me about this factor of the Presidency, I'm not likely to be sympathetic. "You wanted the job, buddy." And while racism has been an unfortunate factor among (Too many) voters; this element being the direct cause of all opposition and criticism against President Obama personally is a myth.

However, most mythology has some basis in fact. In considering this, where does the "Myth" of all opposition to President Obama being racist in nature stem from? Is there, perhaps an underlying racial "Theme" from which the myth draws as its source? In a word: Yes.

Just as the NRA's opposition to President Obama is based on unsubstantiated fear, the underlying racist "Theme" behind some of the more senseless accusations that President Obama either has done or will do is based; not so much on the President himself; but rather what an America that would elect an African-American as President of the United States represents.

In a culture featuring a history almost completely dominated by "White" men, nothing frightens those who believe that they have the "Right" to rule more than a society that wants something that instinctively makes them uncomfortable.

Whether we want to admit it or not, because our entire history has been represented by leadership from the same demographic; and with virtually no variation, anyone coming from outside of that demographic is going to seem, at the very least "Out of Place."

Younger Americans who have seen and experienced African-American leaders ranging from Martin Luther King jr. and Malcolm X and (And this is very important) allowed to continue perceiving them as something "Good" are far more ready to accept the idea of an African-American President; or at the very least be willing to look beyond their own prejudices and preconceived notions than those who, while perhaps growing up at the same time, did not receive the same kind of ideological reinforcement at home.

Cases in point: two kids come home from school and tell their parents that on that particular day, he or she learned about Martin Luther King in school. One kid gets a positive reaction and is therefore that much more receptive to the concept of an African-American as President in later years.

The other kid telling his or her parents and being greeted with a torrent of profanity and Dr. King being accused of being everything from a Communist to a sheep buggerer is an extreme example that might immediately come to mind.

The more likely reaction is something the child would perceive as more reasonable; such as an uncomfortable silence or even a seemingly reasonable explanation of why anyone who isn't "White" is untrustworthy.

The extreme example might cause the kid to roll their eyes and think "Yup...my folks are bigots;" whereas the reaction that seems more reasonable, even while consciously overcome still casts just enough of a shadow of doubt that causes a general feeling that the individual is most likely completely unaware of.

In today's sociopolitical world, what can be loosely defined as social or political reality has been formed through changing racial attitudes that are still in a process akin to metamorphosis. This, I believe has caused an underlying effect of racism that most who exemplify it are not conscious of.

To properly demonstrate this, I think can best be accomplished by using myself as an example. I grew up flooded with negative information on people my own "Race" (for lack of a better word) either distrusted or outwardly feared. Some of these were overt. Some were more subliminal. The overall effect of this left me unconsciously distrustful of people representing demographics that what, I think can only be described "Outside" of my own.

Think of the classic, "Two people walking on the same sidewalk" example. The person who instinctively feels that he or she has something to fear may find themselves crossing the street without even being consciously aware of it.

Similarly, I felt a distrust of people whom the only thing I knew about them was what was outwardly visible, that while not a conscious choice was still racist in its nature; as the only thing I would know about an individual I allowed myself to fear was nothing more than his or her race.

How many times have we heard in our lifetimes, "I'm not racist, but..." followed by something of, at minimum a prejudicial nature; and by people that have come to see as trustworthy?

Most people who may recognize the sound of their own voice saying this may find themselves suddenly not wanting to read any further than this;

and for reasons they don't immediately identify. Something inside of them will tell them to stop; and most likely for a reason their subconscious invents to justify the action; such as suddenly having to go to the bathroom, feeling hungry, sleepy or anything else that seems perfectly natural.

However, what their subconscious is really afraid of is perceiving one's self as racist in a society that views racism rightfully as an absolute evil. As human history has proven from ancient times to today, NOTHING in humanity's narrative has caused more chaos, destruction and horror as racism.

Racism today is less represented by people wearing white, hooded robes or Nazi uniforms; and more by people who rationalize their unconscious racism with reasonable justification. "Why did I cross the street when I saw the black guy on the same sidewalk as myself? (Insert B.S. reason here)." A close second to Racism being culpable for the worst atrocities committed over the course of humanity's existence, is collectively the appalling ways in which the actions of racism have been justified.

Here's an excerpt from a conversation I have actually had. "Why are you so adamant that President Obama is going to try to overturn the Second Amendment? He's never even so much as hinted in any speech or anything he's ever written even implies that he wants to overturn the Second Amendment." Answer: "If you don't believe that he wants to take away our guns, then you're an idiot!" Follow up question: "What evidence do you have that he wants to take away your guns?" Actual answer: "I don't need evidence! You can see it in his eyes every time he's on TV telling his lies!"

That, of course is a more extreme example. More common are people accusing the President of "Lying" while not being able to come up with a single example of a lie; and various examples of his "Liberal Agenda" that the President either has never actually tried to introduce into the legislative process or even mention.

Other examples of an underlying, unconscious racism are accusations of "Incompetence" that don't have corroborating evidence. "Just look at his record! He's incompetent!" There are also the examples of things that have happened that have absolutely nothing to do with either him personally or even his time in office; such as Ted Cruz blaming him for the economic collapse of 2008 that happened two months before the election; accusations of him being "The Worst President in U.S. History" that are stated as fact; but don't feature any evidence; and, of course the latest (At the time of this publishing) having an entire war placed at his feet that he, in fact inherited from the previous administration.

Accusations of being a "Tyrant," a "Wimp," "Soft on Terrorism" and a "War Criminal" all at the same time all point to a general, underlying theme of unconscious racism that is not so much focused on the President himself; but are more based on the overriding fear of a change in culture that the election of an African-American represents.

Of course, President Barak Hussein Obama doesn't want to overturn the Second Amendment! Even Wayne La 'Pierre himself understands this. But what the NRA really fears is that a new generation of American voters might no longer believe that the Second Amendment is worth maintaining and defending. That's the reason for stoking fear. By attempting to appeal to baser instincts and create panic, they wish to reach out to the masses; instead of the intellect of a single individual. In addition, "Maybe he doesn't want to take our guns; but one piece of gun control legislation being passed will lead to a domino effect that over time will eventually lead to the overturning of the Second Amendment" doesn't fit on a window sticker.

Of course President Obama isn't the most "Liberal" President we've ever had! Mitch McConnell sure as hell knows that as he's been in politics to remember just how painful LBJ's handshake was. However, a United States that's ready to elect an African-American man; or worse…any woman as President of the United States is one that might no longer believe in the divine right of "White" men to rule the Earth. That's what keeps him up at night.

While based on some elements of fact, mythology never represents overall truth. While there may have been a war fought between Greek City States against a walled city at the foot of the Dardanelle Mountains that was later and utterly destroyed; that doesn't mean that the city was called Troy, the war was factually fought over a woman named Helen or that a giant horse made of wood was historically built and used by the Greeks to gain entrance and burn the city to the ground.

Myth is, after all a distorted look at facts from a perspective that is favorable to truth. Those who have based their own opinions on either President Obama himself or the factual history of his Presidency on a view seen through lenses tainted by unconscious racism don't have to be openly racist in either ideology or action. They only need to be afraid of an African-American sitting in an office that our previous history had demonstrated for two hundred and thirty two preceding years was the divine right of "White" America to occupy.

Furthermore, it didn't have to be any one particular African-American. It could have been (the male cousin character in Fresh Prince of Bel-Air) and the future he represented would have just as frightening to an established ruling class and those who believe that a world under the control of that ruling class is the way either G-d himself or nature intended.

Richard Nixon Was the Worst President in U.S. History

(Sigh) All I've done is write the headline and I'm already feeling dirty.

There have been more than a few of these little articles in which I've included the all-too familiar phrase, "If you ask one hundred people (Blank), ninety nine will say (Blank)." In this case, however I can use the phrase literally; because I know for a fact that I've asked one hundred people "Who's the worst U.S. President in History?" Answer? Overwhelmingly…Nixon.

If we are to learn anything useful from history, we have to be honest about it. Richard Millhouse Nixon may have been a paranoid, mean-spirited, self-righteous toad of a human being. But that still doesn't mean that he was the worst paranoid, mean-spirited, self-righteous toad of a human being to have ever bugged the Oval Office.

Before we delve any deeper into this subject, it must be observed and duly noted that, although the Senate never got around to convicting Nixon for crimes against the Constitution, the House committee did recommend articles of impeachment be adopted, and the House of Representatives did pass the resolution for impeachment.

In the forty four years since Watergate, the evidence in support of Nixon being aware of, approving of and participating in a policy of political espionage and sabotage against the Democratic Party is all but empirical. In addition, the physical evidence of President Nixon orchestrating a cover-up of the Watergate break-in; including his own voice on tape discussing further payments to the Watergate burglars of up to one million dollars to keep them quiet; and having approved of payments made to those involved in the scandal having already been made, is very compelling.

Virtually all of the principle people involved have confessed to even some of the worst accusations of the policy of political espionage; including G. Gordon Liddy (Who's actually quite proud of himself). Nixon himself confessed in the, now famous David Frost series of interviews.

And let's not forget that he did order bombings in Laos and Cambodia without Congressional approval; and also sent U.S. troops to Cambodia.

All of these are matters of documented facts.

So with all of those horrible things being matters of historical fact, how can one say that he was anything but our worst Chief Executive? Because historically speaking, he wasn't. I think there's a strong indication that he was our most criminal President (Inasmuch as actually getting caught); but not our worst.

Let's take a look at the replay.

John Adams is one of my all-time heroes...but he wasn't really a very good President. He was a great statesman, great administrator, great lawyer...but he didn't work and play well with others. Washington D.C. was burned to the ground on James Madison's watch. Andrew Jackson has been called a "Tyrant" by historian David Ambrose. The entire Nineteenth century was dotted with economic disasters worse than the Great Depression and one can take one's pick of Presidents responsible for that.

Because of Andrew Johnson's vindictive and cruel policies enforced on the South after the Civil War, little boys from Alabama may never hold hands with little girls from Vermont again.

Hoover was an idiot. Truman was a stubborn old goat. LBJ had a great domestic policy; but his handling of both the strategy and politics of Vietnam was appalling. Carter was ineffective as he was unable to work with a House and Senate controlled by his own party; and President George H.W. Bush took the blame for the bursting of the economic bubble his predecessor left him.

And every nineteenth century President has blood on his hands for an entire century of genocide.

One thing that's been almost forgotten by history is the fact that Nixon didn't win the popular vote in 1968. While he certainly and legitimately won the Electoral College, he didn't exactly sweep into the White House with a clear, historical mandate. We still had the most powerful economy in the world. We still dominated trade. The Middle East was quiet for the most part and we had mostly good relations with our European allies. By following the "If it ain't broke, don't fix it" policy that proved successful for

President Eisenhower, I think the argument can be made that he was quite effective in his first term; though his Vietnam policy may have been worse than Johnson's.

And let's not forget that Nixon presided over two incredible events. 1: WE LANDED ON THE MOON! Let me repeat that in case all-caps isn't loud enough for you. WE LANDED ON THE MOON! And you know what else? We brought the people we sent to the moon back alive! And whether we like it or not, no other U.S. President...NONE OF THEM can make the same claim as all of the Apollo moon missions were on his watch.

And he went to China. The way Henry Kissinger would eventually tell the story, one would think that all Nixon did was ride on a plane and smile a lot. But Nixon going to China was tantamount to President Obama crashing Sarah Palin's speech at an NRA convention. It was easily one of the ballsiest things any U.S. President has ever done.

If a traveler from the planet Blorth in the Queequod star cluster were to pick up a U.S. history book and just read about Nixon's first term, said (Undocumented) alien would, I think naturally conclude that Nixon had done a fairly good job in his first term, though with Das Kapital being his planet's sacred text, he might disagree with many of Nixon's policies.

But then there was Watergate. It was an ugly, dark and bitter moment in our history and President Richard M. Nixon is completely responsible for it. His acts were criminal and his abuse of power undeniable.

But was he the worst U.S. President in our history? Hardly. And frankly, I'd rather not discuss who I think our worst U.S. President has been. That's for a different arena.

But before we apply the lessons of history to the future we're moving toward, we have to be honest about the facts of that history as half-truths and misconceptions will only hold us back.

Top 10 Political Myths #8:

President Barack Obama is the Most Liberal President in United States History

Of all the political myths that I have studied, this is one of the more frustrating ones as; despite the relative ease of disproving it, there are still otherwise intelligent people who believe in it. Worse still, even when confronted with critical or even empirical evidence, those otherwise intelligent people will completely nullify the evidence; refusing to even acknowledge the existence of said evidence.

For those people, the following article will be virtually nothing more than blank space. But I'm going to try and get through to them anyway.

To begin, not only is President Obama not the most Liberal President we've ever had; he's not even the most Liberal politician in America today. Political opinions held and positions taken by politicians like Senators Al

Franken, Elizabeth Warren and Bernie Sanders are far more to the political "Left" than anything espoused by the current President.

Legislatures in states like Oregon, Washington State and Colorado have passed legislation that is far more progressive than anything even introduced at the Federal level under the current administration.

Even his signature piece of legislation, the Affordable Care Act isn't really that radically progressive as it supports American corporations and aids in their prosperity. It's good to be a health care provider today.

An attempt to identify the "Most Liberal" President in our history could potentially take us back to George Washington and the Constitutional Congress. It's also possible that we could go back even further to John Hancock who was the President of the Continental Congress that passed our most arguably progressive piece of legislation; that, of course being independence from Great Britain.

However, only going back to the relatively recent turn of theTwentieth Century demonstrates Presidents with far more progressive agendas. Under Woodrow Wilson, women and African-Americans gained the right to vote in Constitutional Amendments backed by President Wilson.

The policy of isolationism and neutrality was contrary to Conservative lawmakers who wanted to join the war in Europe. And, there was of course the OTHER arguably most progressive piece of legislation ever passed; the idea that all of America's social ills could be cured by one blanket law: the total ban of alcoholic beverages in the United States.

How many Constitutional Amendments have been passed in our current decade?

Following a decade of mostly conservative political influence, President Franklin Delano Roosevelt was followed into office by a wave of progressive candidates that passed some of the most sweeping progressive legislation in the historically famous "First 100 Days."

Most of the legislation passed was economic reform and the establishment of regulations meant to prevent another "Great Depression;"

including the establishment of the Securities and Exchange Commission with the purpose of the enforcement of "New Deal" regulations.

There was the creation of the Civilian Conservation Corps (Now known as "AmeriCorps"), the National Forest Service and massive public works programs such as the building of infrastructure in the American South, Hoover Dam and the Golden Gate Bridge that put millions of unemployed Americans to work (So much for government never having created jobs).

And then there were the Sixties.

President Lyndon B. Johnson's "Great Society" agenda is arguably the most progressive series of legislation U.S. lawmakers have ever put forward. Unfortunately, President Johnson will be forever linked with the fifteen year catastrophe of Vietnam, rather than Civil Rights legislation bearing his signature.

Jimmy Carter is a very nice man; he really is. Following the resignation of President Richard Nixon following the "Watergate" scandal, America elected Mr. Rogers. And whether it was flying commercial instead of Air Force One or establishing the Fifty Five Mile Per Hour Speed Limit; it was clear to Americans that he was the real deal.

Under President Carter's administration, government beurocracies grew beyond their ability to be efficient. And although diplomatic victories of a nearly miraculous nature and the appointment of Thurgood Marshall as Chief Justice of the U.S. Supreme Court would be feathers in his historical hat, it can be argued that his focus on Israeli-Egyptian relations took his attention away from pressing domestic issues other than the Fifty Five Mile Per Hour Speed Limit and turmoil in the Middle East.

Is President Obama more liberal than President (Bill) Clinton? That depends on which old man wearing the "Dysfunctional Veteran-Leave Me Alone" baseball cap is holding court at Bill's Grill in Temple, TX (Home of the best Steak-and-Egg Breakfast in the state).

Clinton certainly had more success working with a Republican Congress (That's both houses, by the way). The Clinton Health Care plan failed miserably; and never mind whose fault it was. It just failed. NAFTA was supported by both parties and passed without any real opposition from either side.

It is however notable that after the Assault Weapons Ban passed during the Clinton administration expired under President G.W. Bush, there has been no serious attempt at reinstating it under President Obama.

Jefferson bought us a really big back yard. Lincoln freed the slaves (In the South) and Teddy Roosevelt gave us National Parks and broke up the monopolies. Truman was the first recipient of a Medicare card (Personally given to him by LBJ), Kennedy sent troops to ensure African-American students could go to the same school as "White" kids and even Nixon gave us the EPA. All of these examples are far more progressive both in ideology and practice than any legislation passed on President Obama's watch. In addition, with massive cuts to social programs, dramatically "Right Wing" policies being passed by legislatures in Republican-dominated states and Fox News being the dominant paradigm in "Mainstream" political media, Conservatives really haven't had a lot to complain about in the last seven and a half years.

While Fox News was screaming at people, "He's gonna take your guns...," Republican lawmakers opposed a spending bill for medical services to U.S. military veterans. (Yes...they backed off of that one, but not until after Americans called "Holy Ground Highlander!" on that one).

And...by the way...NOT ONE LETTER WRITTEN ON PAPER EVEN SUGGESTING OVERTURNING THE SECOND AMENDMENT!!!

I hope that clears things up.

Intellectual Cowardice

Here's the problem with "Social Networking." While it does have the amazing potential of being a window on the entire world for the entire world; it unfortunately has been one of the unfortunate causes of the willful ignorance now pervasive in the American political divide.

All the information is out there to make fully-informed decisions about any and all important subjects. But in American political discussion, not only are tens of millions of Americans unaware of opposing political positions or ideology; when confronted with it, they make the willing choice to completely ignore it. Why? Ultimately, it's because they are so absolutely terrified by the concept that if they become simply aware of opposing information, they may actually begin to believe some of it. How else does one explain the bizarre phenomenon of more than two people believing that G. Gordon Liddy is somehow an American hero?

I call this unfortunate element of political ideology, "Intellectual Cowardice." I believe that it's a side effect of social networking as not only does the internet allow one to focus only on political ideology one already agrees with; i.e., "I don't care what the New York Times says, The Village Voice says…" It also allows otherwise intelligent people to completely shut out ideology one doesn't want to read or see; not only by ignoring said information by completely tuning out the sources of such information by deleting sources provided or even cutting off contact completely with an individual providing such information.

"I don't care what facts you give me about the logistical impossibilities of collecting all the privately-owned firearms within the United States. BAN ALL GUNS!! Oh…and by the way…screw you! I deleted your post. Send me another one, and I'll unfriend you on Facebook."

Of course it sounds ridiculous. That's because it is ridiculous! But billions of people all over the world do it every day. Somewhere in Armenia right now, there is a Muslim saying, "Screw you!" to a Christian friend for insisting that not all Christians want to kill each and every Muslim on the face of the Earth. Similarly, I know at least one Texas moron who believes (and this is a direct quote), "I don't care what anybody says. The purpose of Islam is to kill all the Christians in the world. And the next person who tries to tell me otherwise is gonna git a punch in the mouth!" (Source: dumbass in Teddy Bear Bakery, 8:45am, Tuesday July 11, 2016. The first Academy Award nomination for Best Actor goes to the owner of Teddy

Bear Bakery of not giving away the fact that he believed EVERY SINGLE WORD the gentleman said was pure hysterical nonsense.)

The biggest problem involved in this, is that's there no easy solution. It requires more than the changing of American hearts and minds; which has proven difficult at best throughout our history. And it requires more than just the inevitable natural deaths of a few old farts…myself included (There's no way you'll ever convince me that Danny White isn't the greatest quarterback of all time!) It requires every ignorant person in America to make the conscious decision to, at least consider the validity of opposing viewpoints. Trust me…this is not easy.

It certainly isn't natural; especially as even allowing opposing information to get in past the walls we build up over time requires the conscious act of wanting to do so. It also requires that we get over our emotional attachments to what we have come to believe is morally right or wrong. "The idea that Serena Williams isn't the product of genetic engineering to produce a physically and intellectually superior human being is just plain EEEEEVVVILLLL!!" (Vote Sharipova for President 2016!!!)

I have definitely been so cheesed off by the political opinions of some of my bestestest and my closest friends (Are Jewish) that I've considered never speaking to some of them again. This would be a pity, as I owe at least one of them a lot of money and she's certainly not above bringing me before Judge Judy for public humiliation.

But just as having one's own brother murdered by one's most reliable killer is sometimes "Just Business." I feel, STRONGLY that; in politics, it's very often necessary to forming well-informed opinions to give in to our Vulcan side. And to use my faith as a guide, I also believe that one must always be brave in support of one's higher ideals. "All right…I admit. The fact that Serena Williams has normal, human parents is an important factor in her genetic makeup."

After all, completely tuning all opposing information; especially that of a factual nature isn't just ignorance, ultimately it's nothing less than cowardice.

Top 10 Political Myths #7

Social Security and Medicare are bankrupting the U.S. Government

This one goes right along with Social Security and Medicare being "Ponzi Schemes." People who tend to believe this are usually the ones who think that they won't have to rely on either Social Security or Medicare and therefore don't care whether it's there for them or not…until they realize that even with a sixty thousand dollar a year job, they still won't be able to retire until they're eighty…especially with all the credit cards they're maxing out.

Republican politicians hate Social Security and Medicare…until they need money for a war or another tax cut for the rich. Then it becomes their personal Savings and Loan.

It's at this point that I feel it's important that I point out that my singling out "Republicans" for this is less about my personal leanings toward Progressive politics and more out of the observation that the Republican Party no longer represents true Conservative political, social or economic values. They represent nothing more politically, socially or economically relevant than beating the Democratic Party. Obviously, someone (In the comments below) is going to point out that "The Democratic Party is no better." To this, I would argue that the Democratic Party is, at least better at paying "Lip Service" to a true Progressive agenda.

Before I digress any further, I think it's important that I get to the point; and this one is fairly straight forward. Most of the budget for the Federal Government comes from income taxes. Of course there are import tariffs, export tariffs, license fees and other sources from which Uncle Sam draws blood. But the majority of Federal "Revenue" comes from Federal Income Tax. Property taxes, sales' taxes, fuel taxes, state licenses and fees all go to State governments. There are, of course Federal agencies that fund State agencies like Education, Transportation, Health and Welfare

(Which handle food programs); but these Federal agencies do little more than further fund State programs; while occasionally placing conditions on what States have to do in order to further receive Federal funding; such as, "If you want to continue to receive Federal Education dollars, you will adhere to the 'No Child Left Behind' doctrine (Which was thankfully put out of its misery earlier in 2016)."

For most tax brackets, Federal taxes aren't so much "taking" money from tax payers as it is the Federal Government borrowing it, putting it in a bank, letting it accrue trainloads of interest and then paying most of it back once a year. Through earned-income tax credits, deductions for children, charitable contributions and other deductions, some people actually get back more in taxes than they pay. The Federal budget deficit is based not just on more money going out than going in; but more importantly where the money is going; or in the case of the last seven and a half years, where it has been meant to go.

Congress has not passed a budget during the entirety of President Barak Obama's time in office. Why? Who cares? Not important to this topic. What is important is that for seven years, Congress and the White House have had to push through 'Eleventh Hour' spending bills to prevent a complete economic meltdown; while at the same time suffering one government shut down, the gutting of Federal budgets and the downgrading of our national credit rating…NONE of which have anything to do with either Social Security or Medicare.

Why not?

Because Social Security and Medicare are funded entirely by completely separate taxes that are not even supposed to be touched by the Federal government.

The concept is simple. You work. You pay into Social Security and Medicare. It goes into an account that accrues interest. By the time you retire or should you (By no fault of your own) become unable to work, you then draw Social Security in addition to your retirement pension, move to Florida and play golf for the rest of your life. Medicare then takes care of your doctor bills and is supposed to help pay for your medications.

BUT...

President George W. Bush didn't even wait six weeks until breaking his promise to leave the "Social Security Trust Fund" alone. In addition, without having raised taxes to pay for two wars (The only President in our history to do so), even more money was taken out of Social Security and Medicare for immediate budgetary requirements.

Because there are still more Americans paying into Social Security and Medicare than drawing from it and from the interest it accrues from the bank accounts the money sits in, it tends to replenish itself rather quickly. In addition, according to the New York Times, the Wall Street Journal and Newsweek, over forty percent of Americans sixty-five years and older are employed and subsequently paying into Social Security and Medicare. In addition, many retirees who still have their health insurance through their former employers, can opt out of Medicare Part B; which is an extra ninety bucks back in their pockets and millions more dollars going back into Medicare.

The Federal budget deficit has many causes; mostly due to political and economic shenanigans from all sides. Not the least of these shenanigans are that whenever budgets get slashed, Social Security and Medicare are usually right at the top of the lists. Added to that the fact that one practically has to be an invalid to qualify for Social Security Disability AND it being an, at least two year legal ordeal before one sees a single dime; SSDI is taking far less money out of Social Security than retirement benefits; less than twenty percent (Source: Social Security Administration).

Much greater culprits of the current Federal budget deficit are twelve years of "Reaganomics" that (then Candidate) George H.W. Bush referred to as "Voodoo Economics" in 1980 and twenty total years of implementation have taken the deficit to levels that may have previously seemed like Science Fiction had they not become economic fact. In 1980, the word "Trillion" was only a theoretical number. By 1990, it had been far surpassed. Eight years of much more responsible economics left us with a budget surplus by 2000; a surplus that was, once again a multi-trillion dollar deficit before 9/11.

That had nothing to do with the promise this nation made to its seniors in 1933; and neither did our current budget deficit now.

If Social Security is simply left alone and allowed to do what it's meant to do; that is just sit around accruing interest, then the system works. There are those who believe that privatizing it would be an acrimonious solution to those who want to have more control over their retirement earnings. But the best retirement accounts (IRAs 401Ks, Certificates of Deposits, Bonds, etc....) are the ones that are completely left alone.

Even E.F. Hutton will tell investors that the Stock Market is legalized gambling and serious returns require serious investments to begin with. Of course, if one has some form or another of psychic knowledge of what stocks are going to go ballistic within a twenty-four hour span of time or what stocks are going to implode, one can make more dramatic investment decisions, but the Securities and Exchange Commission tends to get a little suspicious when someone gets lucky on a regular basis.

With that in mind, the "Privatization" idea tends to be not very compassionate when Joe "The Plumber" takes out $10,000 from his retirement account to invest in a "Start-Up" that goes belly-up in less than a year. And how many Americans living paycheck-to-paycheck are going to leave their retirement alone when their sewage starts backing up on their front lawn and there just happens to be $10,000 there that they need right then and there.

And what will Mr. or Mrs. America do if the private company that has no regulatory agency responsible for it invests their money and loses it? Now that virtually all of the post-Great Depression regulations have been overturned (And it doesn't matter who's responsible for it), the occasional stock market "Red-Giant-star-down-to-a-black-hole-singularity" collapse isn't so much a possibility as it is an inevitability. Who's Nana going to move in with after her hip breaks and she can't go back to Walmart?

As they exist today, Social Security and Medicare are fine if they're completely left alone. Forty-plus years of economic stability proved that (Twenty in the case of Medicare). But with Social Security essentially being treated by Congress to be "Mom and Dad for when we run out of pizza money," very few people alive today remember what it was like when no one was screaming about Social Security running out, the myth that they are in any way responsible for the American budget crisis is that much

easier to propagate.

Top 10 Political Myths #6: The Poor are Poor by Choice

To begin, I think I should state quite clearly that this is more of a social myth than a political myth. However, as this myth has such a clear effect on American Politics and the distance of many lawmakers from social realities, I argue that including it here is appropriate.

In a word, it' bullshit. The central theme of the mythology is that all Americans are born in an economic system in which every child has the exact same opportunities for advancement as every other child born at the same relative time and; most importantly social class. Example: A kid raised in a Chicago slum has the same opportunity for advancement as a kid raised in a home across the street from the "Collinwood" estate in Newport RI. Nothing could be more out of touch with reality.

Children born in abject poverty in America don't have an absolute guarantee of even surviving past their teens, much less achieve higher economic and social status. The first four generations of Kennedys in America didn't make it out of the Boston gutters, until one of them finally broke the following of the devout tradition of not even touching alcohol accept communal wine and opened up a bar.

Perhaps the best way to illustrate why this ideology is mythological in nature is to take a look at two practical examples: "The kid" raised in an impoverished neighborhood vs. "The Kid" raised in a more "Middle Class" background. Nevermind the rich kids. They're going to private schools, preparatory schools, Harvard, Yale, Princeton…and their families' connections will guarantee them good jobs. They'll be fine.

Here's what the kid spending his diaper days in the projects has to face before even making it to school age. The majority of impoverished children are raised in single-parent homes; sometimes extended family groups if they're lucky. We're still waiting for the proverbial jury to come in as to whether or not the ACA making health care insurance (We'll get to this topic later) more affordable for consumers at or below the poverty line has had any positive effect on the child mortality rate in poor communities; but even these numbers will not change the fact that a child born into a middle income family has a much better chance of reaching the age of six than a child born into poverty. Factors such as crime, unsanitary conditions and less access to a healthier diet contribute to child mortality.

Having reached school age, the Middle Class child has access to better schools which will have an impact on their overall future. The first thing colleges and universities see when a high school student applies for college admission is the names of the previous schools they attended. Even a student who graduates with a pristine academic record at an inner city school is going to be looked at less favorably than a student having come from a more affluent environment. Even a student at a school in an impoverished neighborhood who had straight "A+s" is not likely to impress the admissions department of Texas A&M University, much less Harvard or Yale.

The appalling salaries underfunded public school districts have to offer potential teachers ensures that public schools will not always get the "Best and the Brightest;" and this is especially true in the Deep South (And Texas). These states apply funding according to a neighborhood's property taxes as opposed to distributing funds equally. This is why you have schools like Anderson High School in Austin churning out college student after college student and Reagan High School being a demilitarized zone. And while Anderson can have its "Pick of the litter" in teachers; Reagan is happy to have someone with a pulse in any particular class.

But let's say, just for kicks a student at Anderson and a student at Reagan are both accepted into the University of Texas (The Reagan kid can pretty much forget Ivy League). The first and most obvious hurdle is, of course...how are they going to pay for it? Even state-sponsored schools like UT and A&M aren't free. Full scholarships aren't guaranteed for all "Straight-A Students." Athletic scholarships only apply to athletes who make the cut onto college athletic teams...which is never a guarantee; no matter if one did make "All-State" at Waxahachie High. There are grants out there; but applying for them is a phenomenal pain in the posterior. And all of these examples only apply to tuition. There's still books, supplies, housing and groceries to consider.

That leaves student loans; which even if a college student makes it all the way to a P.H.D or MD is an albatross they're going to carry around for upwards of twenty years. The Middle Class graduate is more likely to find employment with salaries that can make student loan payments more affordable for the graduate from a more modest background that albatross will likely be with them to the grave.

Of course, there's no guarantee that either the poor kid or the Middle Class kid will even make it past their first semester of college. The middle class kid will almost certainly have been to a school that better prepared him or her for college than the poor schmuck. The "Straight-A" student from Reagan is statistically more likely to drop out of college before the end of his or her third semester. The Anderson graduate has a better chance of earning better grades; and of course both may fail for no better reason than they were just young and stupid. However, the Middle Class kid who spent his entire first semester drunk STILL has better employment opportunities than the poor kid who may have failed for the same reason.

The reason for this is the social economic "System" in America is completely unforgiving to the poor. In order to advance economically and socially, a person from an impoverished environment cannot EVER have even one tiny spot on his or her "Permanent Record" during their twenties and thirties.

That means no arrests, no incarcerations, they can't quit good jobs for legitimate reasons such as sexual harassment in the work place (Even if proven to be the victim of sexual harassment, it's still a scarlet letter on one's employment record), incompetent management or inability to work with peers.

The employee from the middle class background is more likely to be given, at least one second chance; and YES, they have a better chance with this if they're "White." I have seen this in my own lifetime; and although it has been to my benefit, I still think it's wrong.

Of course the wealthy will often get all the chances they want, depending on far up the social food chain they are. Of course, now that "Affluenza" is now an acceptable and successful legal defense, not even something as heinous as rape can be an obstacle in the case of someone who comes from an affluent background.

People in lower income jobs are more likely to suffer financially from even the most minor legal offense. Speeding can be a ticket of upwards of $250.00; which is not as much of a burden to someone at a higher income level. To someone earning at or underneath the poverty line, it can be nothing less than devastating.

In Bell County, TX not only do traffic offenses come with a fine, they also come with a mandatory court date. This means that even just running a red light, one will incur court costs; which are NOT negotiable, they can NOT be paid off in increments; nor can they be worked off with community service. Source: ME! This is a process that I'm in the middle of as I'm writing this and for the next 88 days.

After the fines and the court costs, the State of Texas then tacks on a "Surcharge" which is always going to be a minimum of $300. One can pay it off in installments; but they are charged 30% interest and there is even an additional fee if one starts making the payments and then decides to pay it off early. If the surcharge is not paid off by the end of one calendar year, the Texas resident is then slapped with…another surcharge.

If one hasn't paid the surcharge or is late on payments, their license is automatically suspended. I know all of this because, at one time I had five surcharges I didn't know about because according to the Bill written to create this nonsense, the State is under no obligation to notify Texas license holders of having this surcharge. One may get a letter for the first surcharge accrued; but nothing after that.

People in higher tax brackets may not be effected at all by this. The poor will experience sometimes severe hardships as a result of this.

Of course, the above example only applies to drivers in Texas, but every state has laws that inflict more financial hardships on the poor for minor offenses. The accumulations of fines quite often leads to jail time. This leads to time away from work; possibly even getting fired for such time away from work; which, of course makes the poor person even poorer.

So no…not everyone is born into an economic or social class system that is fair for everybody. For every one Julius (Dr. J) Irving who came from absolute squalor and became a millionaire many times over, there are countless millions of examples of people who, though still doing the so-called "Right Things," have not made out of poverty. While there are many examples of people being poor because of one decision after another, this is definitely more the exception than the rule.

Top 10 American Political Myths #5:

To Improve the Economy, We Need to Close the Federal Reserve System

One thing I like to do with the Tastefully Twisted Politics page is disprove the political BS typically found in memes. To me, political memes are yet another example of the existence of pure evil in this world.

What political memes typically do is take bits and pieces of information related to politicians and/or political parties and intentionally distort the facts in a manner that makes the political opponents or perceived villains look bad. A recent example of this is a meme claiming that Clinton family, upon leaving the White House in 2001 "Stole" expensive items of furniture, were forced by law enforcement to return much of the furniture and pay $30,000 in "Fines" and "Restitution."

This is, of course nowhere near the facts of what happened. What actually happened was that when the Clintons left the White House, they did take over $200,000 (Estimated retail value when purchased) worth of furniture; however, most of it was furniture the Clintons had purchased out of their own pockets.

There were, however several items; such as a $60,000 couch, that found its way into the political labyrinth of the confusing nature of the difference between giving gifts to the White House, the office of the President of the United States or the individual person holding that office and/or members of his or her family.

In 2001 (Long before Citizens United), there were strict limits on how much private citizens could donate or give to the individual who works in the Oval Office. There was also a difference between allowable gifts for the individual sleeping in the East Wing of the White House and the office of President; with the limit of giving what is essentially a government employee being the higher of the two.

While most of the furniture was the personal property of the Clinton family, some of it, although given as gifts at a time when people typically receive gifts; i.e., Christmas, birthdays, anniversaries…were in fact purchased either for "The President of the United States," or "The White House." As such they were government property.

When the moving vans showed up, the movers basically just grabbed everything not nailed down and loaded it on a truck. Before those trucks even arrived at the Clinton home, items that were government property were discovered to be missing and it wasn't hard to track them down.

Within less than a week after the mistake was discovered (With the people that the Clintons paid to pack and move their stuff being at fault), almost all of the government property was returned to the White House. Items that were not returned, were subsequently purchased by the Clinton family totaling just under $30,000.

Unfortunately, all that information doesn't fit on a meme in a way that can be read without an electron microscope. Neither does this information fit the political agenda of accusing the Clinton family of being thieves.

These types of memes aren't just factually deficient, they tend to assume that the people reading them are complete gits.

Probably...no...definitely the most outlandish and ludicrous meme I've ever seen featured a photo of Abraham Lincoln with a caption that one of the reasons he was such a great President was that he "Stood up" to that most evil of institution: the Federal Reserve System. The meme actually referred to "The Fed" as being a criminal cartel.

The number of people who believe crap like this because they're unwilling to spend three minutes of their lives doing a simple Google search on the facts of subjects like this tends to result in me brushing up on my conversational German. The knowledge of the masses of people who know next to nothing about the Federal Reserve System or what function it performs doesn't help.

I'll try to be brief and explain the Fed as simply as possible.

Simply put, the Federal Reserve System is the only bank in America that has any actual money in it. Every other bank in the U.S., from the most evil, greedy, criminal organization bank on Wall Street to the not quite as big, but still evil greedy criminal organization bank next door to it, has nothing more than numbers in a computer based on the money in "The Fed." A dollar bill is a piece of paper that is only valuable if there's enough gold in The Fed to cover its exchange value.

There are three Federal Reserve Gold Depositories, located respectively in New York City, Fort Knox Kentucky and San Francisco California. Why three? Why not just have all the gold the U.S. owns in one place? Because the gold in the depositories is the foundation on which the entire American economy is based, they're strategically placed in the two most important cities to the American economy as they are the nation's centers of commerce and largest ports for importing and exporting goods.

The Depository at Fort Knox is in the geographic middle of the United States; presumably safe against the possibility of either a foreign invasion or nuclear strike.

There are three of them based on theory that should something catastrophic happen to even two of the depositories; such as a war, revolution or natural disaster, the U.S. would still have enough money to pay its bills.

This system was put to the test on 9/11. The New York Depository was located directly under the streets near the World Trade Center towers. After the towers collapsed, the Gold Depository was completely cut off from the world above it. Trillions of dollars-worth of gold was completely inaccessible. However, because of the other two Depositories, the economy didn't completely collapse. The system did exactly what it was designed to do.

It's also important to note that the value of the gold is not based on the constantly fluctuating price of gold; but rather on how much a nation that the U.S. trades with would pay for it. One of the results of this is that the U.S. economy is dependent on foreign trade to keep afloat. And this has been a reality throughout our nation's history.

So where did this economical crack house come from? That…is actually a very interesting story.

In 1907, the United States was looking into the face of what might have been the worst financial apocalypse in world history. The greatest industrial giant the world had ever seen and the home of some of the richest people in the world…was broke.

Remember, in the first one hundred and thirty five years of American history, there was no income tax. The previous revenue system of taxing virtually anything and everything that could be bought and sold wasn't cutting it anymore. The still-young nation had become too big for such a tax system to work. In addition, average prices on goods and services combined with taxing every little necessity had gone beyond our collective ability to live in a minimal standard of living. With basic necessities of life taking more than the majority of Americans earned, movement from one wage bracket to a higher one was becoming more and more difficult; nigh impossible if an average citizen didn't start out in their lives close to the middle class to begin with. This meant that, not only would those living beneath the poverty level be cursed to stay there throughout their entire lives, their kids weren't going to be "Movin' on up" either.

With not enough revenue coming in from the old "If doesn't move on its own, tax it" tax system; even with a defense budget less than hundredth of a percent of what it is today (in proportionate dollars), Uncle Sam was busted.

To prevent the complete meltdown of the economy that would have had the effect of the U.S. becoming a third world nation, it had to get a quick transfusion of cash quickly. To achieve this, the U.S. Government, already knowing it was going to have to bite the economic and political bullet of establishing an income tax was forced to swallow even more (Pride) and ask the richest men in America; people like John Rockefeller, Andrew Carnegie and whoever was holding the Vanderbilt check book at the time for a loan.

A lot of the people that the U.S. was holding out its hat for weren't exactly enthusiastically jumping on the "Americathon" bandwagon. For many of them, it didn't seem like an obligation to even lend any of their "Hard earned" money to an economy that collectively had less money than only one of them. Who cares how many kids are starving in the streets? If it doesn't directly affect me, I don't care.

This is where one of the most colorful people (Man or woman) in U.S. history comes in. I am, of course referring to James Pierpont Morgan.

J.P. Morgan wasn't nearly as rich as men like Carnegie or Rockefeller. However, it wasn't the money he personally had that gave him almost god-like financial power. It was the money he controlled that made him powerful.

Morgan was an "Investment Banker." An Investment Banker is someone who invests money into people or organizations in exchange for profiting off the money the individual or organization made and a measure of control over the individual or organization. Before 1907, Morgan financed men like Thomas Edison, Alexander Graham Bell and even a young John D. Rockefeller. He also invested truckloads of money into banks and in doing so gained control over them.

The more money one invests in a bank, the greater amount of control one achieves. By 1913, Morgan was the CEO of, at least 20 different banks in America. Many of the so-called "Robber Barons" of the late-19th century that owned over 90% of the total wealth in America (Not an exaggeration. It might be debatable now, but it was a cold, hard fact back then) had money in the banks he ruled. As such, with their money in his fist, he was a virtual dictator over the entire U.S. economy.

Truth be told, he was an arrogant, heartless, greedy son of a bitch who wouldn't have given up a nickel if his own mother were about to be kicked out of her nursing home. But one thing he did understand and was able to communicate to his fellow arrogant, heartless greed sons of bitches was that if the U.S. were to go bankrupt, neither he nor anyone else with a mansion in Newport, Rhode Island would have any money at all. Nothing...zero...nada. If the U.S. went broke, so did everyone else.

A great story about the negotiations for the filthy rich to loan America money is that, after arguing back and forth for weeks, no deal had been struck. This is when Morgan gathered all the bankers and corporate Czars into one room, locked them in and wouldn't even leave to go to the bathroom until a deal had been made.

A deal was struck in less than seven hours.

One of the most important elements of that deal was the creation of the Federal Reserve System; and by partnering with the economies that feature similar reserve institutions; such as The United Kingdom, France and Switzerland, and basing the value of the gold in the System not on the often wildly fluctuating price of gold, but on the more consistent amount of how much another nation would pay us for our gold, it ensures relative stability in the national economy.

Think of it as sort of despite being relatively financially secure, knowing from experience that one's finances could potentially collapse at any moment, as they may have done so before. In preparation for this possibility, you've taken such precautions as purchasing something of a comparable value and isn't going to depreciate very much over time and is something that, in a pinch can be sold for a quick infusion of cash.

When the Jews were being kicked all over Europe by...whoever was persecuting them at any given time in history, they often invested in gemstones; such as diamonds, sapphires, rubies, etc. Having already been forced to pack up and move over the course of 2,000 years, it probably didn't take long for Jewish communities to figure out that it was always a good idea that if the government of the nation in which they were residing woke up one morning and decided to seize all the land and property of Jews within their borders...again, they would have something of value that they could trade for currency. This is a historical practical example of keeping something safely tucked away that virtually anyone would be willing to pay money for, should the need to sell it raise its ugly head...again.

So now the Fed's starting to look better and better. Why would anyone want to change that?

For one, most Americans have never been fond of the idea of someone else being in control of their dough. Another factor is that the Fed is very strictly regulated and harder to manipulate from the outside.

The result of earning higher actual dollar amounts with the easing of regulations may seem attractive; easing restrictions of how much currency is in the open market at any given time devaluates the currency as a whole.

This is why old paper currency in America is regularly destroyed with new bills replacing the old. If the U.S. Mint didn't destroy old bills; that would mean more bills circulating in an economy in which the value of the currency steadily begins to fall. If there's $1 trillion worth of gold in the depositories, it's not a good idea to have $2 trillion dollars in circulation.

This also feeds into the myth that the Fed arbitrarily decides when to raise or lower Federal interest rates on savings, investments, bank loans, personal loans, business loans...anything that changes the value of money currency represents. This myth would have us believe that interest rates are determined by a committee. Interest rates are the result of the ratio of the physical amount of currency in circulation to its corresponding gold in the Depositories. The Fed doesn't so much dictate interest rates in America as it essentially just tells Americans what it is at any given time.

Finally, the Fed is often unpopular because of the perception that it limits the dollar amounts one can potentially earn. This is...not a myth. That is precisely what the Fed does.

Although there is a lot of it, what we perceive as "Money" is a finite resource in a closed circulation system. And as with any other finite resource, the more one individual or group has, the less another individual or group has. By strictly controlling how much currency or credit is in the open market at any given time, it prevents the U.S. from being in a situation like pre-revolutionary France and Russia. In both those cases, with a tiny minority controlling and keeping almost all of the money in their respective economies in their own pockets, the economies and social structures of the two nations completely collapsed; resulting in some very hungry and very pissed off citizenry. "Anyone who doesn't eat for three days can become a revolutionary: Vlad Lenin."

Many politicians on both sides of the political aisles don't like the Fed because the government has absolutely no say in how the Fed is operated or in the decision-making process of Federal Reserve authorities. The Fed may as well be its own sovereign nation. There is also the perception many have of the Fed's officers hoarding all the money in America and not letting anyone else get near it; and I think with the appalling wage gap the nation has today, Americans have a legitimate beef.

The Federal Reserve System was inspired by an economic disaster and with the primary purpose of, no matter how bad the American economic system got bitch-slapped, there would still be enough hard currency for the U.S. as a nation to pay its bills and maintain the circulation of currency within said economy. As Americans have proven time and time again that pure greed prevents the American economy from stabilizing itself.

What we saw in 2008 was the result of the American market not regulating itself as Alan Greenspan predicted (And then later had to eat a huge platter of crow in front of the entire nation). With the Federal Reserve System being the only financial institution that has real money in it, it is still absolutely essential to our overall economic health.

Top 10 American Political Myths# 4

The EPA is no longer necessary

One really can't have an honest discussion about the Environmental Protection Agency without at least mentioning one of the greatest ironies in American political history: The EPA was created under the administration of President Richard Nixon. Yes...THAT Richard Nixon.

And no...it wasn't a case of the bill creating the agency having so much support in Congress that they could override a Presidential veto. While the Democratic Party did have a "Super-Majority" at the time, the creation of the EPA had more than enough bipartisan support to have been passed even with a perfectly "50/50" split of Democrats and Republicans. In addition, a possible Presidential veto was a non-issue. I'm not even sure Nixon read the bill before signing it.

The typical American image of the EPA has no better been represented than in the (Original) film "Ghostbusters." The 1984 classic film introduced us to the character of "Templeton Peck;" who was essentially an unrepentant, capricious, ball-busting prick who may have likely been taking his revenge on all the kids who bullied him by being the biggest unrepentant, capricious, ball-busting prick he could possibly be.

The irony here is that the EPA arguably does have the largest supply of unrepentant, capricious ball-busting pricks of any institution in the world. But the formative first decade of the EPA's existence arguably created an easily understandable philosophy that this is what would be necessary in order to do their job. After all, the EPA wasn't exactly brought to life in an era where environmental concerns were of particularly high national concern. This was an era when simply tossing one's trash out of the window of one's Dodge Charger spewing black smoke from its 4.50 liter, solid lead fueled engine that got 7 gallons per mile was generally preferable to having trash clutter up the car's all-important back seat.

This was also the era in which corporations like U.S. Steel, Ford, General Motors and Chrysler were still the most profitable corporations in the world. Not only did these corporations and others like them have lobbyists with deep pockets, (Just like today) there was no shortage of politicians reaching into those pockets. This factor makes the very creation of the EPA that much more miraculously ironic.

I guess they thought the EPA was just planting a few trees.

In that era, "Beta Tester" EPA representatives didn't exactly make one phone call to Kaiser Aluminum, ask them nicely to cut down on dumping toxic waste into Lake Michigan and then see Kaiser happily comply. With most of the first EPA representatives having already run screaming from their offices with their dreams shattered, the ones that stayed realized they were going to have, not only get dirty themselves; they were going to find more people like Templeton Peck.

If one really takes an honest look at what the EPA was able to accomplish just within its first two decades; especially considering who they were up against, words like "Incredible," or even "Miraculous" are perfectly appropriate. Considering the monumental task set before them to take half an entire continent that looked like a teenager's room and make it presentable to visitors again, there simply aren't enough superlatives in the English language to properly give an idea of the Red Sea the EPA parted.

And this brings up a problem that younger politicians and those who are politically active face today have. They lack perspective. In 1970, even Ann Coulter might have looked out her penthouse window and said, "We've got to do something about this." Most people under thirty five don't remember pushing six-pack rings out of the way when swimming in a lake; nor do they remember having to pull "Pop Top" can tops buried in their profusely bleeding feet on the beach. By not seeing how bad it really was for themselves, it's almost impossible for many to imagine how bad it could get again were it not for the EPA using Draconian methods today.

So the EPA accomplished a Herculean task in the 70s and 80s. That's great! But surely we don't need the EPA anymore…right? Nobody throws ten pound bags of trash out of their car windows anymore...do they?

Just as in the EPA's infancy, it's not that which could easily be seen that was the problem; neither was what had already been done the biggest challenge facing the agency today. Asking John and Jane Q. Public to stop tossing their trash into a lake was easy. Asking U.S. Steel to add filters to their smoke stacks to prevent acid rain was another challenge entirely.

In the 70s and 80s, the war between EPA and major manufacturing was vicious, dirty and one in which actual lives were lost (See: Karen Silkwood). Passing environmental regulations was the easy part. Enforcing the laws is, even to this day a struggle greater than the Rebel Alliance vs. the Galactic Empire.

With the EPA having recruited a staff of the most surly, insecure "I'm-going-to-make-the-world-pay-dearly-for-my-suffering" Americans they could find and corporations fighting back with often unspeakable acts of evil (See: Karen Silkwood), it was as nasty as nasty gets.

Worse still, it really wasn't a fair fight. Instead of Capitalism vs. Communism, a better analogy might be Israel vs. the entire Middle East. A relatively small U.S. Government regulatory agency vs. the largest, most profitable corporations in the world (At the time) was, and arguably still is David vs. Goliath and his army of lawyers.

Again, the victories the EPA did win are akin to climbing Everest with one's shoelaces tied together. But even the fights the EPA won are relatively easy compared to what the EPA faces today. Not only do they have to fight tooth and nail against corporations today; they also have to fight against a public with little or no perspective of the challenge before them.

"What challenge" you ask? Didn't the EPA win the environmental war? Didn't we save the Spotted Owl? Earlier this week, I called the EPA's public information desk and asked if they could give me a rough estimate of fines that the EPA have had to impose in just this calendar year alone. Because much of what I asked represented cases still in court, they couldn't give me a solid number. However, I did manage to get a concession that the amount for 2016 was "well" over one billion (U.S.) dollars. Not only are we only in August (At the time of this publishing); that approximate figure only represents the violators that were caught.

And although the EPA couldn't give an accurate dollar amount of fines imposed or being litigated, I did get a straight and clear answer to the question "Has there been a year in which the EPA has not prosecuted a U.S. business for violating environmental law?" That answer was an unambiguous, "NO."

The argument against the EPA is the same as its always been. They're bad for business. They restrict free enterprise. And, of course those supporting this theory point to the demise of corporations like U.S. Steel and the "Big 3" auto makers. However, more likely culprits of this are competition from Asian markets. The same nation that won WWII with considerable help from U.S. Steel now buys most of its metal from China. As for the "Big 3," instead of blaming the EPA, one might look more at American auto manufacturers making shitty cars for the better part of four decades.

So yes…we still need the EPA. If the U.S. were to go one single year without any U.S. businesses getting fined for environmental infractions, even I might begin to think that the EPA could start letting up on the thumbscrews.

But even factoring in completely accidental environmental infractions, someone having the job of investigating and determining the difference between environmental accidents and intentional lawbreaking is absolutely necessary.

And "Who ya gonna call" to clean up the occasional spill of toxic sludge? That's right. The EPA is responsible for cleaning up when corporations refuse to pay.

"Surely not," one may say. "No American institution is callous and inhuman to refuse to pay their fines or clean up their messes when caught red-handed." Really? Exxon is still fighting the fines imposed from the Valdez oil spill.

It would be great if we lived in a nation where big business operated under the philosophy that the environment was important enough to fit into their overall financial strategy. However, it is historically clear that the

sacrament of this Kool-Aid is one that is still being refused.

Top 10 Myth of American Politics #3

Someone who is successful in business will be equally successful in

political office

I would like readers to take note that I was very careful in the way I

worded the title of this myth. I did not write, "Someone who is successful in

business 'can't' be successful in politics…;" I specifically wrote, "Someone

who is successful in business 'will' be successful in politics." There's a

subtle, but rather profound difference in "Can't be" and "Will be." And it's

that difference that defines the myth.

In our history, we have yet to see a successful business person be

elected President. In fact, I'm pretty sure that the only example of anyone

who had "Ran" a business ever becoming President include Harry S.

Truman…and he was a dismal failure at it.

Teddy Roosevelt had also tried his hand in the corporate arena...and was a dismal failure at it. And President George W. Bush's corporate resume isn't particularly impressive either.

So there's no real historical precedence pointing in any direction of the possibility that a successful business person "Can" be a good politician at any level. However, the myth is that one can assume that someone who succeeded in the corporate world "Will" be successful. While there's no empirical evidence whether or not a successful person can do well in political office; the implication that one can assume that a successful business will be effective in political office is unfounded.

Why not?

The corporate world and the political world are two completely different environments. Corporations have a hierarchal structure in which those at the very top of the corporate hierarchy can dictate policy down through the ranks; but not vice versa. While the CEO of a corporation can certainly tell the 18-year old kid who just started in the mail room to get him or her a cup of coffee; that same 18-year old would have to ask the CEO very politely for a cup of coffee.

And while the CEO can, with the support of a board of directors dictate company policy; for example…the dress code of the corporate headquarters; unless that dress code has legal flaws in it; such as women being required to wear revealing outfits, there's nothing anyone in the mail room, no matter how long they've been in the mail room can do or say about it.

In a corporation, an employee can be fired for any number of legal reasons. Example of these include: consistent failure to show up for work on time, failure to adhere to the (Legal) dress code, insubordination or just good ol' fashioned incompetence. In addition, even a member of the Board of Trustees (Board of Regents, Board of Elders…) can lose their job if the other members of the Board agree. Even Donald Trump could become unemployed if a majority of the Board of Directors at Trump Hotels and Casinos votes to remove him from his position.

That's not the way things work in government at any level.

Most people in government positions are elected by a majority of registered voters in their precinct, ward, city and state. The only government position reliant on a majority vote of the entire nation is the office of President of the United States.

There are positions related to government in which people can be "Appointed;" such as Cabinet positions, Judges in certain states (In Texas, Judges are elected), Supreme Court Justices and other similar positions; but the person(s) in seemingly higher positions of authority can't just fire them for any reason.

In the rare circumstances that someone in these kind of positions have demonstrated a need for them to be removed from office, they technically can be "Fired;" however, the elected official seeking to fire them has a very narrow set of criteria under which the individual can be fired. A historical example of this is when President Richard Nixon attempted to "Fire" the U.S. Attorney General, the U.S. Supreme Court essentially vetoed the firing. Similarly, elected officials can ask political appointees to resign due to the same reasons a person can be fired from a business. However, if said appointee refuses to resign, the elected official who had appointed the person in that position is then stuck with having to fire the individual within the narrow criteria.

So unlike a CEO being able to say "You're Fired" and the person having been told this instantly being unemployed, people in government positions aren't that easy to get rid of.

Similarly, in a corporation, those who are in positions of authority can dictate policy down through the hierarchal structure in a way that government office holders can't. Obviously, the CEO can make and enforce blanket policy that applies to the entire corporation. But in addition, lower level management can create policy over their own area of influence; so long is doesn't conflict with the overall policy set by those higher in the corporate structure. A CEO, with the approval of the Board can dictate that all employees have to wear Campbell Tartan plaid every Thursday; however, a lower level manager can't contradict that policy by creating a policy that says, "Screw the CEO! All employees must wear Stuart Tartan plaid every Thursday."

And, of course neither one of these examples of policy can be enforced if either Tartan isn't specifically issued to employees by the company or if obtaining the Tartan is in any way unreasonable. A company can create and enforce a policy that employees must wear steel-toed boots because steel-toed boots are readily available and can be obtained in virtually any conceivable price range. However, that company can't create or enforce a policy that states that all employees wear complete and authentic Star Wars Stormtrooper costumes as they are not readily available; nor are they cheap.

In the structure of a Democratic Republic government, the President of the United States cannot dictate absolute policy. Even an Executive Order can be overturned by the Supreme Court if the Order can be argued to be Unconstitutional.

Using the "Dress Code" example again, the President of the United States can't create a Dress Code; nor can Congress pass any law that enforces one over city, state or federal elected officials. They can over government employees; such as...an 18-year old in the mail room. However, such policy can't be created or enforced over other elected officials.

Similarly, whereas the kid in the mailroom has absolutely no say whatsoever in a legal and reasonable dress code having been set as policy by any level of management all the way up to the CEO; a "Freshman" House Representative can show up in a pink tutu and, so long as that's not the only thing he or she is wearing; nothing can be said or done about it. (Incidentally, both the U.S. House of Representatives and the U.S. Senate do have dress codes that have been set through the legislative process; but are extremely flexible. Our "Freshman" House Representative doesn't necessarily have to wear a jacket and tie; but he can't show up dressed as Dr. Frank N. Furter from the Rocky Horror Picture Show either)

In addition, if policy in a corporation is being considered that the kid in the mailroom objects to; unless the policy is somehow illegal or violates his civil rights, he can't really do anything about it. If the board adopts a policy that he has to wear a tie at work every day, guess what... he has to wear a tie every day. In a representative government however, if the freshman House Representative doesn't like a policy being considered for any reason, he can hold up the entire legislative process by way of a "Filibuster." Think Ted Cruz reading a children's book as part of hours and hours of filibustering. The kid in the mailroom can't do that.

This is why I often find myself laughing whenever I read or hear political candidates criticize opposing candidates for being, "Career Politicians." For one: being a "Career Politician" isn't inherently evil. Two: it sometimes takes "Freshman" Representatives and/or Senators a year or two find out where the bathrooms are in any given capital building or courthouse; much less be effective. And finally: what the hell is the person accusing the "Career Politician" doing? Perhaps City Council members or elected members of the District Board of Education are going to keep their day job. But someone running for the U.S. House or Senate is certainly looking for a career change. And what's going to happen to that farmer, plumber, teacher or kid in the mailroom after he or she has been in political office for ten years? That's right... he or she becomes a career politician.

And don't try to tell me that anyone who runs for political office any higher than Comptroller just wants to do that for a couple of years and then go back to selling used cars.

The bottom line is that being successful in business and being a successful politician require two very different sets of skills. The CEO of a major corporation doesn't necessarily have to work and play well with anyone outside the Board. A politician has to be able to network, coordinate and work with people; no matter if they personally like them or not.

First they must take on the challenge of learning to work with the established office holders in their own political party; and then maybe after the ten years it takes to achieve that goal, THEN he or she has to learn to work with people on the other side of the political fence. This couldn't have been easy even in the rare times in American history where political rivals were working toward the same goals (Example: winning WWII). In today's vicious political climate, being a bloodthirsty tyrant isn't likely to work out very well.

The final nail in the coffin of this myth is that the Constitution of the United States was specifically designed to avoid a hierarchal structure. Unlike corporations, the real political power in the U.S. Government is spread evenly through the three branches of government; each one being able to overcome the power and influence of the other branches. Congress can pass a law, but the President can veto said law. And even after the President vetoes a law; if a bill has enough support from the entire Congress (How often has that happened), a Presidential veto can be overridden. And no matter what Congress or the President do considering any piece of legislation, the Supreme Court can still say no. This is almost, but not quite the polar opposite of the way corporations function.

Again, I'm not saying that a successful business person "Can't" be an effective legislator. However, the reason why politicians tend to be better suited to holding elected positions is that the skill set of a politician is better suited to being a part of a government that operates efficiently and effectively. Even the President of the United States has to be able to talk to the Speaker of the House without it turning into a fist fight.

I am definitely of the opinion that one of the biggest culprits guilty of our current governmental dysfunction is that there aren't enough "Career Politicians" in elected positions. The very concept of politics is being able and willing to work with people whose views and positions on a variety of subjects and projects are different than one's own. I think the best analogy of this comes from (Former) House Representative Barnie Frank. Before retiring, he explained that when he perceived as the time when the U.S. Government was working best, "We'd have all have our own views and say things in front of the cameras; but in the end, we'd eventually sit down, break out the cigars and the Scotch and make things happen."

In recent years, the offices in the government requiring elected officials have demonstrated to be better with politicians manning the helm; rather than having someone coming in without the intention of working constructively with others. The attitude of "Now that I'm the boss, you're all going to have to do what I say," may work well in the corporate level; but the last twenty years of American history has shown that in government, it does not.

Top 10 American Political Myths #2

President Bill Clinton Was Impeached for Cheating on His Wife

Some may be disappointed by this myth's high ranking; especially those ready to do battle over "Trickle-Down Economics Actually Working;" which, I believe history has clearly proven false. I'm pretty sure that only the most devoted conservative sheep continue to believe that one. As such, it no longer has a real impact on American politics today.

What earns this myth its high ranking is the rather sad picture it gives of how woefully uninformed the American public is about a subject that should be important enough for Americans to, at least try and have informed opinions about. Alas, politics and how it effects the everyday lives of Americans is sadly not important enough to everyday Americans to research beyond the memes that appear on their newsfeeds on Facebook; or at the very least fact check what their favorite politicians say in public. If they did, we might still have a government that functions.

But I digress…

Already

Of all the political myths covered in this series, it should be the easiest to disprove. After all, President Bill Clinton was not impeached for having his "Cigar Smoked" in the Oval Office. He was impeached for having lied about it under oath. While both are examples of pure stupidity on the part of an otherwise intelligent man; only one of them is actually illegal.

Most people either aren't aware of or remember the ridiculous circumstances under which the impeachment process was brought about. Even those who were alive and politically active at the time far too often weren't paying any real attention to what brought about this moment of history. They're not consciously aware of how the situation was brought to public light in the first place. The two idiots on "Friends" making every single mistake one can make in a relationship was far more important. Similarly, the supposed "Immorality" of President Clinton's administration was more important than a steadily improving economy and a stronger dollar against foreign currency provided by President Clinton's economic policies. This gave us the Republicans' "Contract with America;" which twenty two years later, they have still not fulfilled (How many Republicans running on "Term Limits" are still in office?).

What follows is as brief of an overview of the history of the Clinton scandal as I think can be presented. In 1993, the Department of Justice began investigating possible malfeasance between the law firm Hillary Clinton had once been employed at and the Whitewater real estate firm she had formerly represented. With "Whitewater-gate" beginning to cast a shadow over the Presidency, President Clinton appointed a Special Prosecutor to the investigation, Kenneth Starr.

Wise choice or not-so-wise, that's a subject for another debate. The historical fact is that Starr proved to be nothing short of a virtual "Pit Bull" in his investigation. Even well after no malfeasance was discovered in "Whitewater-gate," he continued to investigate every little detail of the Clinton administration that could possibly be considered unethical or immoral. Between 1994 and 1998, new political "Scandals" were "Uncovered" by Starr's committee, eventually leading to over three hundred million dollars spent by Starr and his political wolf pack.

Although all of Starr's committee's "Scandals" proved to be wild goose chases, he kept bringing up new ones so regularly that ending Starr's investigations couldn't be stopped in any way that wouldn't make the President look bad or lead to "Obstruction of Justice" charges. And no matter how utterly ridiculous the accusations may have seemed either at the time or in retrospect, calling a halt to Starr's investigations would have made the President look guilty of, at least unethical behavior.

In 1998, Starr and his committee hit pay dirt. They uncovered a rumor that President Clinton had a physical relationship with a White House intern named Monica Lewinski; a name that would become so much part of the English language that the version of Microsoft Word I'm currently using knows the correct spelling (In addition to most of the Star Trek lexicon).

So Starr and his team sunk their collective teeth into the rumor and, not only did they find corroborating evidence to support it, including physical evidence, they discovered that it was something the President was likely to lie about.

This is where I skip to what is referred to in the Porn industry as the "Pop Shot." The President was subpoenaed and…like an idiot, he refused citing Presidential Privilege. The Supreme Court ruled that Presidential Privilege didn't apply and President Clinton would have to give testimony in deposition.

So the President sat down with Starr's prosecutors and was asked about the affair. Like an idiot...he lied...under oath. Whether he was being questioned about receiving oral sex from an intern or selling arms to Iranians to financially support covert operations in Nicaragua wasn't important. He lied under oath and Starr's committee had more than enough evidence to support an indictment.

From there, the process moved so fast, people's heads are still spinning. From indictment to a vote on the House floor to impeach was less than three months; and this is where a historically monumental occurrence happened. Despite overwhelming evidence, the vote to impeach barely passed with House Democrats and Republicans voting along clear party lines. What proved to be deciding factor in the House vote was the Republican majority in the House. This was much different than President Nixon's impeachment which had decisive Republican support and a vote that wasn't even close. Since that vote, nearly every Congressional vote has been a clear case of Republicans and Democrats voting on party lines, instead of voting according to the merits of the bill. For seventeen years, legislation has been decided by which party holds a current majority; and not the merits of the actual legislation brought to a vote.

The next step was up to the Senate. According to their vote, President Clinton would either be convicted of a crime, removed from office and hauled out of the White House in handcuffs or finish his term as President of the United States. In this circumstance, the vote from the Senate needed to be more than a simple majority. With Senators again voting along party lines, the conviction did not have the prerequisite percentage and, therefore did not pass. President Clinton finished his term arguably on good terms; but also with an undeniable stain on his time in office.

Personally, he was barely skinned by the incident. He obviously wasn't thrown in prison. Commanding six to seven figure speaking fees and having received an unheard of ten million dollar advance on an autobiography that is still the biggest selling autobiography ever printed, he's earned more money than he's ever made in his political career. So, it looks like he's done rather well. In addition, his own personal scandals either in office or out of it haven't appeared to have a significant effect on the career of the only woman in the world who wouldn't have divorced him and sued him for every penny he was worth after finding out he cheated on her.

But still, they myth of him being impeached because of the affair persists. The myth has earned its place on this list because of the impact it still has on the political opinions of a public too intellectually lazy to make sure they're fully informed about political fact vs. myth before making their selection in the voting booth.

Sad? Yes. Frustrating? Definitely. Easily fixed? Please! If politics isn't important enough for Americans to try and get more than one side of a political topic now; what makes anyone think it's even possible to change? People like…well…me will continue to try, but I doubt me or anyone else will see this even begin to change in our lifetimes.

What is "White?"

In my writing of any nature; political, social, entertaining, amusing, crushingly depressing; I've often taken risks and chances that my family and fiends tend to think of as "Unwise;" perhaps even dangerous. But hey! I'm a writer. It's what I do.

More than that though, I tend to see my scribblings as being of a kind of "Spiritual" nature to the point of having a nearly religious attitude toward it. Even the stuff I intend to be funny (and usually fail), I take very seriously. I take it so seriously in fact that people who have known me (literally) for decades are surprised that I take anything as seriously as my work. Hell…most of my fiends are surprised I take anything seriously at all.

As previously stated, I've taken some chances with my writing that many have felt to be "Ill-advised." However, if there's going to be one thing I've written (And subsequently made publicly available) that might get me killed, it's going to be this one.

Yes, I know I've ruffled some proverbial feathers in the past; and to be perfectly honest…yes…I have often enjoyed it.

However, when one gets into any subject that comes anywhere even in the same zip code as race, one instantly becomes "The Tooth Beaver;" chomping and hammering away at the single tastiest part of the human body: a nerve ending.

Even now, I can see the rose on the television screen, hear the tolling bell, the steam escaping from…somewhere, see my favorite horror film character and hear him say in his ultra-creepy, distorted voice happily announcing "We have such sights to show you."

Ironically, I'm not worried in the least about how my "Rainbow Coalition" of Freunden will view what follows. It's the "White Supremacist" out there who will accidentally happen on this chapter and decide that I'm the guy that G-d has been commanding him to kill all along.

So let's get right down to it, shall we?

Here we go!

What exactly is "White?"

I sincerely hope I've established having the reputation of someone who does, at least the bare minimum of research before putting my non-fiction out there; so I'll skip the full report on how I've been bugging the people at the public library and asking them the question, "What is 'White'?"

Answers have typically ranged from strange looks, unsettled expressions and library security asking me to please not bother people anymore. I've also asked this question, not only of my family and fiends; but also relative strangers or casual acquaintances. But even among the people who strain against the restricted space of the heart that I've crammed them all into, no two answers have been the same.

I, of course asked a sociology professor at THE University of Texas at Austin (Hook 'em Horns). I think there was good information in her answer... tough to tell though. She said a lot of words... a rather hefty serving of words.

I've asked Priests, Rabbis, even one of the Romani men that live around the corner. Got another strange look.

And I did some serious research as well. I called the Southern Poverty Law Center in Georgia, The New York Times Public Information Desk, sent an email to "The Onion" (Which is if responded to by the time I publish this will be included. Cross your fingers folks), asked a Social Worker at the Texas Health and Human Services Commission (AKA: "The Welfare Office.") Heck... I even sent an email to Al Sharpton (No response at time of publishing). Alex Jones hasn't returned my call.

And yes...I even called who should have been the undeniable experts on the subject of race; that of course being the American Knights of the Ku Klux Klan, the Church of New Enlightenment and the Texas offices of the American Nazi Party. I got some information. Oh boy did I ever get some information! But even these stalwart institutions couldn't seem to agree on one, solid definition.

The Southern Poverty Law Center gave the general definition of "White" as being "Of European Descent." However, the AKKKK (I wonder if they ever really considered what an acronym of their name would look like) disagreed...rather strongly. According to the AKKKK, not all people of European Descent fit the definition of "White." Scandinavian descent? Yes. English? Germanic (German, Austrian, Dutch)? Hell yeah!

Scottish? Mmm...maybe. No really...that's precisely what the guy on the phone told me. Irish? No! That's correct, according to the spokesperson for the AKKKK, the Irish are not "White." His exact definition of where the Irish should sit on the racial bus was...not language I like to publish; at least in non-fiction anyway.

The American Nazi Party did acknowledge Irish heritage as fitting the criteria of "White;" but curiously enough, only Irish descendants of Americans. When I asked the spokesperson if this meant Irish immigrants who had interbred with Native Americans, she hung up on me. It was one of those old fashioned phones too; the ones that make that definitive "CLICK" when slammed down.

By far, the absolute best was the Neo-Nazi minister (After convincing the receptionist that I was working on a serious article about racial origins; which required explaining to her what the Ahnanehme of Nazi Germany was…more on them later), he explained to me in great de-tail how the "White" or (A word I will use rather frequently from now on) "Aryan" race were direct descendants of Adam and Eve whom G-d had placed in the Garden of Eden and all other races were subhuman creatures that had been created by Satan; specifically for the purpose of "Destroying G-d's racially pure world by having those of inferior races forcibly interbreed with Adam and Eve's pure Aryan offspring."

I SHIT YOU NOT!

Of course, when it comes to "Scholarly" research on racial origin, no one did it better than the Nazis…the real ones; not the guys involved in a rather twisted version the Society for Creative Anachronisms.

One element of the Holocaust that is frequently either misunderstood or just completely ignored is that the institutionalized racism inherent in the Nazi Party didn't just pop up in the late-1920s. Nazi racist ideology was the product of centuries of racism that, left unchallenged had developed over the course of generations from simple irrational prejudice to a pseudo-scientific philosophy widely accepted, not only as fact; but also the product of legitimate, academic research.

Culturally speaking, Pre-WWII Germans were very studious intellectuals who valued the organization and "Comfort" of a well-ordered society. They still are, for the most part; but before WWII, German culture was a lot stuffier than it is today.

Prior to WWII It was contrary to German nature (And yes…I'm well aware of how this sounds like racial profiling…and yes, I'm giggling at the irony of it) to believe in anything that wasn't supported by solid documentation. In Pre-War Germany, it wasn't just enough to claim that Jews were subhuman to make Krystallnacht justifiable. To convince Pre-War Germans of anything, it had to be proven. To get past the perfectly organized beaurocratic German defense against BS, there had to be some way to back up any kind of claim; no matter how ludicrous or reasonable what's being presented as fact may be.

Fortunately for Hitler and his cronies; and specifically SS Chief Heinrich Himmler, they had a centuries old tradition of Antisemitism to work with. In addition, they had some otherwise highly intelligent people who were more than willing to intellectualize racism to the point where it seemed perfectly reasonable.

By the 1930s, there were "Scientists" who were considered experts in "Race." There were "Professors of Racial Studies." And in 1933, Himmler brought many of these people together and gave them real money to work with. This would be the creation of the "Ananehme;" which was a quasi-academic department that was not part of any "Official" government agency; but rather came under the umbrella of Himmler's SS. Being under Himmler's direction was important as it meant that the head of the SS and the Gestapo could maintain control over it; and ensure that it did what he wanted it to do.

The primary purpose (Publicly at least) of the Ananehme was to conduct scientific and academic research into the individual, human characteristics of "Races" and cultures. Under Himmler's direct control, it very quickly devolved into Himmler throwing tons of "Reichmarks" into the effort of proving even the most sickening racial stereotypes to have 'some' basis in scientific fact. The end result would become nothing less than warped ethnic myth and complete fabrication presented in such a way to give the illusion of respectability. Think AKKKK with a thesaurus.

By starting from the theoretical basis of the existence of the godlike "Aryan" race and given the mission of discovering the geographical origins of the Aryan people, Himmler's Ananehme weren't so much given a general idea of where to find the evidence to prove the factual basis of their theories, as they were GPS coordinates. Himmler essentially dictated to the "Academics" working under him, "This is where the Aryans come from; go find me any scrap of information that can logically be used to prove it." By 1938, the Ananehme was about halfway up the Himalayas in search of Aryan ancestry that Himmler knew could only be found in the factual location of "Atlantis" (Not a joke.).

The "Atlantian Theory" of the origin of the Aryan race is neither the only theory of Aryan origin; nor is it the most interesting or entertaining. It is however, the most common.

The theory goes something like this. Ten thousand years ago, while the rest of humanity was still following herds of Wooly Mammoths around, there was a race of godlike, super humans living on the island continent of Atlantis. After Atlantis was destroyed by...something, there were some survivors that migrated first into the Indian subcontinent; and then later finding their way into central and Northern Europe.

Somewhere in this story, a very important element of Nazi racial ideology occurred; that being the capture of Aryan women and the forced interbreeding with Jews. By intermingling "Impure" and "Inferior" blood, the Aryans were brought down to the racial level of the rest of humanity and; while still being fundamentally superior, were no longer godlike in nature.

This mythos served two important functions in Nazi ideology; establishing a basis to support the theory of German ethnic superiority and creating a historical and cultural antagonist having sinister plans that have to be defeated. Both of these would lead to the justification for one of history's most horrifying atrocities; one that the Nazis honestly believed would be remembered by history as something fundamentally "Good."

During their search for Aryan roots, the Ananehme would go on to creating what could possibly best be described as a racial "Scale;" which naturally featured Aryans at the very top and Jews at the very bottom. In between these bookends though, was a gradually descending scale of; what I suppose could be referred to as "Whiteness" that categorized Europeans in different regions and cultures according to an arbitrary set of standards.

It's important to note at this point, that the criteria used to classify this graduating scale was not so much pulled out of thin air as it was centuries of beliefs about the superior/inferior nature of differing cultures in the vastly diverse European cultural makeup.

These differing peoples and cultures, I believe can best be compared to kids who spend their entire lives living on the same street. They grow up together and are so familiar with each other that they essentially develop into a kind of warped, but semi-functional family unit. A case in point that I believe might demonstrate this point is that the concept of the European

Union may be based on the notion that Continental Europe has always had a kind of shared culture; and more importantly, an interdependent "Web" of trade and culture.

Hidden beneath that cheery image of the happy European "Family" is the very real nature of cultural differences which had, for centuries led to mistrust and cultural tension. And while sharing a lot of similarities, there were just enough cultural differences for beliefs of superior or inferior nature to develop.

The scale the Ananehme developed was reflective of this. While Scandinavians, Germans and English were higher on the racial scale; Italians, Greeks, Spanish and Portuguese were lower of course.

Lower still were Eastern Europeans; such as Hungarians, Czeks, Bosnians, Croatians, Romanians and, of course the Russians.

Curiously, SS and Ananehme archival information doesn't feature a lot of information about people of Celtic origin (Scottish, Irish, Welsh); however, the Ananehme research projects were still incomplete when interrupted by the rather inconvenient World War that became the priority in Germany.

What all of that boils down to is that even the nation and culture that undoubtedly spent the most time, effort and resources into the research and classifications of races, did not clearly define the nature of "White." By the twentieth century, the idea of German and English cultures being closely linked was generally accepted in both Germany and England. This is in a very large part due to the cultural and historical reality that the first major immigrant group to settle the formerly Roman province of Britannia were Germanic Saxons. The native Celts and Angles may not have been thrilled about it; but it happened nonetheless.

The Ananehme would also categorize the French higher on their "Racial Scale" than most other people and cultures in Europe; but they were still rated lower than Germans, Scandinavians and British; in that order.

The British too had their own historical search to prove that their general theory of "Whiteness" had some scientific and/or academic basis. While readily accepting Charles Darwin and his origin of species theories, the English were still generally uncomfortable with the idea of all humankind originating in Africa. This would be a major factor in the

"Piltdown Man" hoax having been so quickly embraced and even stubbornly defended as fact for as long as it was.

English notions of "Whiteness" were based less on the totality of contributing factors such as nose size, brow size, differing shades of eye color (Which the Ananehme did significantly contribute to scientific research by discovering over fifty different shades of eye color.), differing shades of skin color; and more on the less tangible aspects of how superior British culture was to the rest of the world.

Beginning sometime in the late-seventeenth century and lasting approximately until just after WWII, the British had developed the idea that theirs was the most advanced and most "Civilized" culture in the world; so much so, that they saw themselves as having the responsibility of essentially civilizing the rest of the world.

Perhaps the best evidence of these ideals can be found in the document "White Man's Burden" by Rudyard Kipling. In in, Kipling clearly voices the British philosophy that it was the "White Man's" responsibility to bring the rest of the world out of the sociological "Dark Ages" and into modern times; whether the rest of the world wanted it or not.

This philosophy would manifest itself in ways that ranged from fairly interesting; such as enforcing English standards of dress in places like Australia…in the summer, to one of the most bizarre and radical "Eugenics" experiments in history. That being the attempted selective breeding of Australian Aboriginal females with "White" males; which in theory would lead to the complete breeding out of inferior racial distinctions in four to five generations (See: 2001 film "Rabbit Proof Fence").

But as to any kind of logical or rational means of defining the general idea of "Whiteness," the British only generally associated skin color with cultural inferiority or superiority and more on what they saw as the tangible elements of what they perceived as "Modern." One example includes, the British demanding that the Zulu King Cetchuwheyle cease following the tradition of marrying girls as young as fifteen or sixteen to men as old as thirty-five.

Of course when this demand was officially made in a letter from the British Viceroy in Natal, it was just a reason to go to war with the Zulu and take their land. However, research through British newspapers and literature at the time has demonstrated that this practice was something the British viewed as inferior in nature; even to the point of Queen Victoria writing a letter to the British Viceroy in Natal asking if there was anything he could do about it.

The British classifications of "Whiteness" wasn't as organized or classified in as much detail as the Germans either; and remember, Nazi ideology was originally a twisted, perverted, extremist ideology that did have its roots in basic German culture.

Of course the British, the French and the Germans were "White." But what about Italians? No. Greeks? No. Eastern Europeans? Do you means "Slavs" or Russians? Russians yes. Slavs no.

Scottish? They're coming along. We'll soon have them civilized. Irish? Certainly not!

Of course if there were any classifications either then and/or now that ever agreed on anything regarding the question of what is "White" or not, it was that Africans and Jews were most certainly NOT "White."

The Nazis saw the Jews at the very bottom of their ascending/descending scale; whereas the English considered them as "Tolerable" (One could, after all do business with them, invite them into your home, perhaps even have them involved in government); and so long as they knew and respected their proper "Place," they could be allowed to remain in the same company as "White;" but never actually become "White."

Both the Nazis and the British historically agreed that Africans were not only not "White;" but that they were essentially not even human. As Darwinism was becoming the predominant intellectual paradigm in British scientific and academic circles; the scientific and academic establishment of England wasted no time in defining "Negro" as being lower on the evolutionary scale than "Homo Sapiens."

The Nazis believed that Africans were animals and even as late as 1994, there were Germans who believed that African men and women had tails.

And so…after seventeen pages and three thousand words, we come back to the question: What is "White?" If one is looking for a "Textbook" definition based on clearly defined criteria…sorry. You'd likely have better luck looking for a fully illustrated Dr. Suess book that explains where babies come from.

The basic concept of "Whiteness" would seem to have less to do with skin color and more to do with how a culture views either itself or others within arbitrary criteria of superior or inferior.

What history has shown us is that the very concept of "White" is based on the principle that people originating from differing demographic backgrounds are inferior or superior to one another based on factors that are either unclear or completely beyond even the very concept of logic. The notion of the inherent quality or lack thereof of humanity being defined within strictly defined categories has never proven to have any historic or cultural merit. However, just as everything else related to the topic, no ideology doesn't have to make any sense to be adopted or held as "Truth." It only needs to fit into a worldview in which some believe their rightful place is to be in control'; whereas others are meant to 'be controlled'.

And here it is folks!

Your number one American Political Myth!

Liberal Bias in the Media

"If you tell a lie often enough, eventually people will begin to believe it…" Josef Goebbels.

Not only is this the most familiar political myth in America; and indeed the world, it's also the oldest. Most politically active, or even politically interested people tend to think of this as a notion that is specific and particular to the American media; however, its origins predate even the very concept of European colonies declaring their independence from their "Mother" nations; such as England, Spain or Portugal.

Going all the way back to days of Gutenberg, the established European nobility feared that the sudden availability of the written word and the information contained in those words would serve a "Liberal" social agenda that would upset what they felt was "The Natural Order;" in which their right to rule came from nothing more meaningful than the acknowledgment of their births. In fact, the politically dominant European Church passed an edict that all printed and published Bibles were to be written in nothing but the Latin Vulgate that was essentially the unofficial official language of the Medieval Latin Church.

For the record, I don't like to refer to the Pre-Reformation established church as "Catholic;" as the modern Catholic Church bears only a passing resemblance to the Church Martin Luther was pissed off at. Let's just say they've worked out a few "Kinks" since then.

Ever since the dawn of what one could loosely define as a "News Media," it has been accused of serving a mostly progressive political and social agenda. Following a peasant uprising in the Holy Roman Empire in 1512 (in a region that is now part of modern-day Germany), Martin Luther blamed what was considered "The Media" at the time for having stirred up revolutionary sentiment; and even recommend that the established nobility of the region destroy all printing presses in the region. This, they quite happily did as part of a rather brutal answer to the uprising.

Of course, what turned out to be even more effective was for the established ruling classes to gain control of a medium that was still in its infancy. The media was a very long way from being where it is today; an entire universe unto itself where any kid with a laptop, a Wi-Fi hot spot and a dream could become the next William Randolph Hearst (We'll get to more about him a little later). Printing presses took up entire houses and the task of printing up one single page of any document was tedious and physical labor.

To legally print anything, one had to have a license to do so; which could only be obtained through the local, gentry-controlled government; which of course had final approval of all material to be made publicly available.

While there were rare examples of activist groups operating printing presses in secret, they typically didn't last very long. Printing presses and the much friendlier to the established order material they produced were much more common. Combined with literacy becoming more common in Europe as a result of a rising middle class, continuing to print what the established order approved of became much more profitable as well.

The American Revolution is often cited as a "Smoking Gun" of progressive bias. This is based on the perception that all or most of the newspapers printed and sold in the American colonies were in favor of either the very idea of independence or the revolution of the time. This isn't even close to accurate.

Maintaining a newspaper or any other form of printed media hadn't become any simpler since the days of the Gutenberg Bible. The only real difference between medieval printing and the American Colonial era is that with the printing industry having matured into a very profitable industry, those who operated printing presses could afford to hire people to do the less glamorous work for them. This meant they could produce more printed pages, charge more money, earn more money; and thus an industry began.

While revolutionary fervor was definitely stoked by progressive media sources; it's completely inaccurate to say that the overall media of the colonies was slanted away from British rule. During the Colonial era and even during the Revolution, the British maintained strict control over all print media and exercised that control with rather brutal force. Hundreds of Americans were imprisoned or executed for the crime of operating a printing press without a proper license. In addition, according to University of Texas history professor Dr. Richard Ryan, for every one newspaper that was friendly to the idea of independence, there were likely six that continued to operate even after the revolution that were not. One example of this was the Boston Gazette; which all the way until the War of 1812 advocated for reconciliation with Great Britain.

One thing that the world seen through our perspective often overlooks is how Earth-shattering the very concept of a press without government control was in the late-eighteenth century; much less how revolutionary that concept still is to this day.

From 1512 to today, there has always been the idea that if left without any controlling influence, the news media would naturally gravitate in a "Liberal" direction. It is for this reason that the most oppressive governments have always made a point of exercising the strictest control over all forms of media; news, fiction, non-fiction; all the way down to children's entertainment.

Even in modern times, a news media or "Press" without some kind of government control is a rare exception. In so-called "Social Democracies" like Germany and France, most news media outlets; while still being corporations have their governments as major shareholders of the corporation and this also includes controlling and regulating influence.

In addition, these nations feature legislation that restricts their media outlets in ways that would cause Alex Jones a horrifying death. For example: in the Federal Republic of Germany, advertisers cannot refer to their competitors by name or use anything that resembles their "Corporate

Property." Burger King cannot claim to make a better hamburger than McDonald's, nor can they display an image that resembles "The Golden Arches," "Ronald McDonald" or even a photo of something that looks like a "Big Mac."

Similarly (And you're going to love this), politicians cannot criticize their political opposition personally. They can't refer to opposing candidates by name and can only make general claims against political platforms or ideology. In addition, they can't refer to opposing political parties by name in the context of criticism. They can only go as far as saying, "Our policies are better than theirs;" and that's it! They can't even say why their policies are better.

But even these "Far Left" methods of government control over the media; that essentially mean that everyone involved in political discourse has to play nice in the sandbox are still based on the same operating theory; that being that government maintaining some control over the media is necessary to prevent opposing ideology. With no control over the media, there is no control over what ideas get spread, right? Yes... Europe has some baggage from its rather colorful twentieth century.

This is where the era of the "Corporate Media" comes in. And yes...this is where our old pal William Randolph Hearst comes in.

William Randolph was the son and heir of millionaire and U.S. Senator George Hearst; who also owned the San Francisco Examiner. After inheriting a sizeable fortune and a small newspaper, Hearst relocated to New York; where he promptly purchased the struggling New York Morning Journal newspaper; and so began his evil plot to dominate the American news media by using the "Liberal Media" to manipulate how innocent, unsuspecting Americans thought.

At the very least, that was the accusation leveled at him by the wealthy, "Robber Baron" clique he managed to piss off while in the process of building a media empire that included twenty eight newspapers across America.

While W. R. Hearst may or may not have liked the actual nuts and bolts of running a daily newspaper, he became particularly enamored with the incredible power that running a newspaper gave him. For some time in the Morning Journal's early and rather lean years of being run by Hearst, he discovered that by simply manipulating the wording of a particular story, he could in fact change the way people actually thought about it.

The classic example of this is, of course how Hearst was able to take the historical non-issue of alleged Spanish atrocities on the tiny island of Cuba and turn it into the Spanish American War. Fresh from this success and still flush with more cash than the entire Catholic Church, Hearst set about the task of shaping the collective mind of America by buying up as many newspapers he could get his greedy little hands on. And while John D. Rockefeller watched his Standard Oil broken apart following the successful prosecution of Anti-Trust legislation, Hearst guaranteed total control over his newspaper empire by funding the campaigns of friendly politicians on both sides of the political aisle.

Historical note: in one of the greatest historical ironies in human history, by maintaining stock in all of the companies that Standard Oil was broken into; including Esso (Exxon), Mobile, Standard and about a dozen other subsidiary corporations, Rockefeller saw his own personal wealth grow from a pedestrian (Just over) two hundred million dollars to over a billion dollars in less than five years. Previous to that, the number "One billion" was only a theoretical number.

Back to Hearst…

When it came to liberal ideology, Hearst was; publicly at least the proverbial "Real Deal." It's very likely that had he the chance, he would have gone to people's homes himself to collect their guns…with every cameraman he could find strategically placed like snipers. Single-Payer Health Care in an era before an income tax? He actually advocated that it was government's "Moral Obligation."

In the late-nineteenth and early-twentieth century, Hearst would go on to purchase and outright own twenty eight newspapers across America; and Hearst was far from being averse to using his newspapers as a "Bully Pulpit." With this being used as "Solid Proof," the accusation of "Liberal Bias in the Media" started rearing its ugly head again; and with the evidence being Hearst's control over twenty eight newspapers in major U.S. cities.

The argument went something like this, "The news media is liberally biased; because William Randolph Hearst owns twenty eight newspapers across America."

Hearst newspapers were especially critical of established political office holders and candidates for their overt corruption Why hide it? It's not like anyone was going to do anything about it. The Democratic Party's Tammany Hall political machine in New York State was the best political system money could buy and the hoarding of wealth was also something that they also weren't bothering to hide.

However, with Hearst newspapers criticizing the political establishment; which was indicative of both political parties at the time, the thousands of newspapers in hundreds of cities all over America were lumped in with Hearst in the all-too familiar accusation.

The solution to this was to control what all the other newspapers in America were saying. How would corporate investors and the politicians they kept in their pockets accomplish this? Simple: buy the newspapers criticizing them and the political engine they merrily supported, fire the people who had been the most vocal critics and replace them with writers and editors guaranteed to present a softer image of corporate America.

Instead of being a greedy ogre who ensured his workers lived in abject poverty and made them work fourteen hour days in deplorable conditions; Andrew Carnegie was a "Captain of Industry" who gave jobs to the huddled masses who were poor by choice to begin with anyway.

The Suffrage Movement wasn't brave women facing horrifying brutality for daring to ask for one simple degree of the basic dignity men were naturally entitled to. They were ungrateful, brutish, probably lesbian women who wanted to make hardworking men their cowering slaves.

Factory workers were barely human brutes who were likely to bring down all the higher principles of the good, clean society the wealthy had been so magnanimous in giving us. If they want to be able to afford more bread, they should work more hours, right? That's how you take a dialogue between management and labor and turn it into a war with real violence and casualties.

Children who are responsible enough and brave enough to work in horrifying conditions should be rewarded with hard-earned pennies; not packed up, sent to an establishment specifically designed to brainwash them and indoctrinated with liberal, Anti-American ideology. That's how you justify children as young as four working in, getting permanently maimed or killed in factories; and this is precisely the world view that corporate newspapers were promoting to a public that even if they could read only had these points of view presented to them.

And it should be noted that this was an era in which the "Print Media" was at its most dominant and influential. It wasn't like today where major cities like New York or Chicago have a handful of newspapers competing with each other, while the vast majority of cities and towns in America had only one. At one point in time, New York alone had over a hundred newspapers operating at the same time.

In this era, population centers that had only one newspaper were, most likely little more than rustic villages with reporters writing about which wall the village idiot fell off of. In 1910, the little town of Elgin, TX had a population of just under three hundred…and it still had the Elgin Courier.

Hearst's own political ambitions were stifled by political machinery that played the games of corrupt politics just a little better than he did. Although he did serve New York State in the House of Representatives, he lost two elections for Mayor and, quite famously a nearly successful bid for Governor.

By 1925, Hearst still owned twenty eight newspapers in the United States; all of them dutifully towing the same line. And while Tammany Hall Democrats were still swimming in cash given to them directly by wealthy contributors, Republican candidates adopted a much more effective strategy of shaping the framework of political debate through buying up as many newspapers as humanly possible.

All of this was long before regulations passed in 1933 prevented private or corporate ownership of more than a maximum number of "Media Outlets." Most newspapers in America would come under the control of banks and corporate underwriters who allowed the newspapers to operate "In House" but with managing editors and senior editors who were selected at the corporate level.

At this time, Hearst newspapers could shout "Corporate-Owned Media" all they wanted. With as many as ten other newspapers in the same city shouting him down, Hearst's political influence was all but gone by 1925; mostly due to the power of a Republican Party that, in the era of Prohibition no longer even pretended to be interested in any constituency other than big business.

Don't believe me? Then spend a couple of weeks going through the archive sections of public libraries and read articles from corporate-controlled newspapers of the era yourself. It usually takes progressives who accept this challenge less than one day to become nauseous with the way the supposedly "Liberal Media" slathered over their corporate masters. Conservatives take a little longer.

To be "Fair and Balanced," the Republican Party of the early twentieth century and up to the election of 1932; for all intents and purposes no longer exists. Pretty much all of the corporate puppets of Pre-Depression U.S. government were voted out of office in a political brushfire that practically no incumbent survived.

But I digress…

Did the Stock Market Crash of 1929 bring this to a screaming halt? The era of "The Great Depression" and a Democratic Party sweep of the 1932 elections might give that impression. However, while many corporations and Hearst did sell off the majority of the newspapers they owned; they maintained controlling interest in the media empires created in the wake of the collapse of the privately-owned news media: The Associated Press (AP) and the United Press International (UPI).

Instead of owning or controlling individual newspapers as the Hearst Corporation or the corporations that opposed Hearst had previously done, the stock holders who had gotten mega-rich from the profits of the near-monopoly of the American news media used the exploding technology of wireless radio to create two central news agencies that disseminated news and information to news media franchises that would contract with the AP and UPI for news from outside of their local domains. To get news from New York, the Austin American Statesman contracted with the AP. To get news from Chicago, the Dallas Morning News contracted with the UPI.

And all the franchises contracted with the AP and the UPI got their news from what was referred to as "The Wire;" a constantly streaming source of news and information operating twenty-four hours a day, transmitting news stories from across the entire nation; and eventually the entire world; first by telegraph, but then eventually using further developed technology. You know those little machines, covered in glass domes, spitting out "Ticker Tape?" That was "The Wire;" and after 1930, two…yes two U.S. corporations transmitted all news and information over it to every newspaper, radio station and eventually every television station in

America…and the people who sat on the Boards of the two corporations were not exactly the founders of the Green Party.

As previously stated, part of the mythos of "Liberal Bias in the Media" has always been the notion that, if left to its own devices, the media would naturally lean to the left without conservative control. Since the very first printing press first spat out its first auction list, the most conservative elements in a given society have either maintained what they believed to be their rightful social and political control by controlling the media; or by claiming "Liberal Bias in the Media" whenever they receive any degree of criticism.

Pope Innocent IX proclaimed that the printing press was a tool of the devil in promoting thoughts and ideas that were meant to overturn the natural order of the world guaranteed by divine right. Martin Luther blamed the misuse of the printing press for a peasant uprising. Mary I of England had all printing presses outside of London destroyed as they allegedly were being used to fuel Anti-Catholic sentiment. Don't ask what happened to the people using them. Just imagine the worst and realize that you're probably not even halfway close. Little Sister Elizabeth was just as unfriendly to a free press and just as brutal in putting it down.

Sir William Pith (The Younger), Prime Minister under George III blamed an English-based "liberal" press for being the root cause of the revolution in the Colonies; but not oppressive taxes, no representation in English government and (The final straw) trying to take guns away from those same colonists. It seems that's always been a sore issue.

Andrew Jackson blamed a "Liberal Press" for Indians daring to fight for the land they'd been living on for ten thousand years. Southerners, of course blamed a "Liberal Press" for anti-slavery sentiment; but ironically, Northern politicians also blamed a "Liberal Press" for promoting a false image of slavery as being somehow moral; as at the time, morality and political idealism based on religious conviction as opposed to the rationality and reasonability of practical political ideology was, at the time considered "Liberal."

Woodrow Wilson blamed the "Liberal Media" for essentially creating a Civil Rights "Concern" where there had been none before; in addition to calling for the U.S. to enter WWI. Point of fact, Hearst-controlled newspapers were clamoring for U.S. involvement in the war; but arguments can be made that this was more due to the German munitions market drying up after 1915 (Before that, "Neutral" U.S. weapons manufacturers were happy to sell to "Huns" and Brits alike); and W.R. Hearst just liking to stir stuff up.

President Herbert Hoover blamed the "Liberal Media" for over-exaggerating the minor economic crisis that would become "The Great Depression." And ironically enough, FDR blamed the conservative-controlled "Conservative Media Bias" for the National Recovery Act being shot down by the Supreme Court.

With the AP and UPI having complete and absolute control over the news media just before, during and after WWII, the very idea of a "Liberal Media" was so ludicrous, not even Macarthur made a real effort to use it during his little "Tussle" with President Truman. But that didn't stop Thomas Dewey from blaming a media that overwhelmingly adored him for his loss.

When pressed for evidence of the historical "Smoking Gun" of "Liberal Bias in the Media," most believers in this mythology naturally point to how the Civil Rights Movement was presented in the media. However, what can be argued this instead demonstrates is a factor of the American media that Dr. King understood, but George Wallace clearly did not. After WWII, and having to feed a public starved for the same kind of daily human drama we'd come to crave, the news media became attracted like mosquitos to electronic bug zapper machines to more and more sensational stories that produced greater levels of shock to the American public that was increasingly getting harder to satisfy.

In a biography of Rosa Parks written in 1974, she mentioned that there had been incidents of her not giving up her seat well before her famous incident; however, the press didn't take notice of it until she was arrested for it. Similarly, there had been non-violent resistance to Segregation and peaceful demonstrations in the South that hadn't garnered any real attention from the American media since the end of WWII until somehow a photograph of an African-American man being attacked by a police dog made it out onto "The Wire." After that, television news crews now having the technology to capture visual images of news stories in real time and spread them all over the nation, found their way to the South hoping to get footage of another African-American being brutally denied his or her civil rights or human dignity. For this, the Chief of Police in Selma, Alabama was happy to oblige. Never mind the woman in Selma who had been turned away from the County Registrar's office seven times after not passing "Citizenship Tests" including questions like "What was the name of Andrew Jackson's dog?" The supposedly "Liberal Media" didn't care about progressive sociopolitical ideology until tear gas pellets were fired into crowds and heads were cracked open by police batons.

Since the 1960s, we haven't had a "Liberal" or "Conservative" media as much as we've had a news media desperately searching for the next shocking story that's going to earn someone a few statuettes on their desk. The "Watergate" story never appeared on the front page of the Washington Post until White House staff started responding to it. And how many hippie communes were out there virtually ignored by the "Liberal Media" before Jonestown? "U-bar-U Ranch" in Texas is a communally owned and operated religious-themed retreat center operated by UU churches running it cooperatively for twenty years. Never heard of it? That's probably because they haven't found 900 bodies strewn all over the grounds.

How many peaceful college campus protests were there before Kent State? How many successful missions with zero casualties were executed by the FBI and the ATF before the Branch Davidian Complex? The last launch of the Space Shuttle Challenger was being broadcast on CNN because a previously scheduled press conference had been postponed. After that, CNN had live coverage of every Space Shuttle launch...just in case. Similarly, CNN had almost never broadcast Space Shuttle landings before 2003; and they certainly never followed a Space Shuttle launch for three hours with a camera focused on a spot where a piece of debris was most likely to cause potentially fatal damage.

If there really was any sociopolitical bias in the media at all, it certainly has neither helped nor hurt either political party. (Then) Former Arkansas Governor William J. Clinton was a political nobody, until the same rabid media wolves that had successfully destroyed the campaign of Michael Dukakis reported that Clinton had an affair with a secretary named Jennifer Flowers. From that point on, the only things that seemed to matter to Americans about Clinton was that his wife was hotter than Barbara Bush and that Arsenio Hall let him play sax with the band.

Not even accusations of poor management leading to failed businesses or drug use had any effect of either of President George W. Bush's campaigns and the allegedly "Liberal Media" didn't sway the balance of a close election in Al Gore's favor.

I firmly believe that the only people who really care about American politics are the people who vote in mid-term elections; both of which were brutal on President Clinton's administration.

"But what about the media drooling over Barak Obama?" How many African-American Presidential candidates that weren't complete political morons had there been before him? Jesse Jackson? Al Sharpton? And even among those who ended up voting for him were less concerned about his political agenda and more attracted to the perception of his campaign being a sociopolitical movement akin to the Civil Rights Movement itself. That looked much better on a TV screen than a "Tin Man" who chose an imbecile as a running mate.

In addition, this "Drooling media" hasn't done him a lot of favors in the mid-term elections; especially with the dominant voice of American political information being the unabashedly Right-Wing Fox News. With Fox having a larger market share of American viewers than all of their competitors COMBINED, it seems rather clear that all that media inundation from the naturally liberally bent "Main Stream" media may not be quite the information flood the myth of "Liberal Bias in the Media" would have us believe.

The history of the news media has been one dominated by the fear that any method of putting out information that is not strictly controlled is going to be used to overturn a firmly entrenched political establishment and social class structure; and the ways in which those representing that established system have used their wealth, power and influence to maintain control over the way social and political discourse are framed.

In the long history of the media from the first printing press to Alex Jones, examples of true progressive political and social ideology being even fairly represented in the media are extremely rare. Much more common are examples of the manipulation of the media by those with an agenda contrary to progressive ideals to misrepresent opposing ideology to such a degree as to make it look ridiculous.

How many people "Educated" on "Mainstream" media can explain what "Redistribution of Wealth" means, other than walking into a rich person's home, taking all of their possessions, cashing them in and giving the money to the poor? Yes…people believe this. That's how a mostly conservative dominated news media can convince an American audience of the existence of a "Death Tax."

How many people are still urging people to purchase health insurance policies from private insurers INSTEAD of signing up for "Obamacare?" And how many hundreds of tiny, startup health care insurance companies have popped up flying banners outside their strip-mall offices that read "Sign up for Obamacare here!"?

And where could one look for accurate information about the Affordable Care Act? An "Infommercial" might help, right? I'll bet the "Liberally Biased" media shows it at "Prime Time" on television every night, right? Nope. These usually get thrown in with the rest of the late-night programming; such as "Infommercials" about health care providers like "Humana."

"Look at how the media is supporting Hillary Clinton!" Show me one newspaper headline, magazine article, website or even a political meme that says, "Hillary Clinton is NOT a liar!" If she is elected President, Time Magazine will likely have her on the cover along with the headline, "Woman of the Year." Time Magazine has had the winner of every Presidential race as "Man of the Year" since the Stone Age. President George W. Bush was "Man of the Year" twice; so was President Obama.

"Look at how the liberal media has crucified Donald Trump!" Today on CNN, Donald Trump's face was shown for over one hundred total minutes before three-thirty. Hillary Clinton: less than one minute total.

The myth of "Liberal Bias in the American Media" is based on the concept of a press completely free of government control would naturally gravitate to the political and social "Left." However, there has never been a time in American history when the American media has been completely free of some form or another of conservative control.

In Colonial America, it was the control of the British Government. After Thomas Payne published "Common Sense," he was imprisoned and his printing press destroyed. Benjamin Franklin largely stayed under the British media radar by publishing most of even his politically motivated literature as satire that the Crown didn't get. And for every one newspaper printing press destroyed by the British and editor hanged, there were more than a dozen newspapers that remained open for business by not pissing the "Mother Country" off.

In Post-Revolutionary America, only the wealthy could afford to operate and maintain a newspaper. Civil War-Era media was historically dominated by both the North and South accusing one another of the opposing media of being "Liberally" biased against them. Post-Civil War-America saw the dawn of the Corporate Media and the Great Depression saw the dawn of the AP and UPI monopolies.

Civil Rights Activists and other "Liberal Agitators" couldn't get anyone's attention unless there was a local government official stupid enough to use violence.

Today, the media is dominated by whoever yells something loud enough and "Interesting" enough to catch someone's attention. Today's media isn't representative of ideologies or agendas. Its stupid people posting their kid slamming head-first into a Semi on a skateboard on YouTube and Breibart resurrecting a story about a Secret Service agent complaining about how cold the White House is and turning into "Shapeshifting…Reptilian…Aliens…in the U.S. Government." I only wish that were an exaggeration.

The myth of "Liberal Bias in the Media" is the product of the fear of a truly liberal news media, what damage it could do to a solidly entrenched social and political establishment and the absolute necessity of preventing that from happening at all cost. This is just as true today as it's been since the first Guttenberg Bible was bound in leather; and so long as there are people in positions of power and influence afraid of what a truly free press might say about them, they will always do whatever they can to control the way political and social discussion is framed. And with regulations limiting how many media outlets can be owned by one person or corporation having been overturned, the Rupert Murdoch's of the world can, once again dominate the discussion by framing arguments in a manner that is favorable to the way they want others to think.

The American News Media has always had an agenda; but historically, it's been one dominated by profit and controlling a commercial market much more than political ideology. The corporations who control the American media today have two major concerns: maintaining influence over the political discussion; getting people to buy the products advertised in between updates on the Malaysian airliner that is still missing.

The media gravitating to political "Left" is something that's been feared since the first buffalo was drawn on a cave wall; but so long as there's somebody that has one dollar more than anyone else, we're not likely to ever see whether it actually happens or not.

www.ingramcontent.com/pod-product-compliance
Lightning Source LLC
Chambersburg PA
CBHW070140290526
45789CB00002B/565